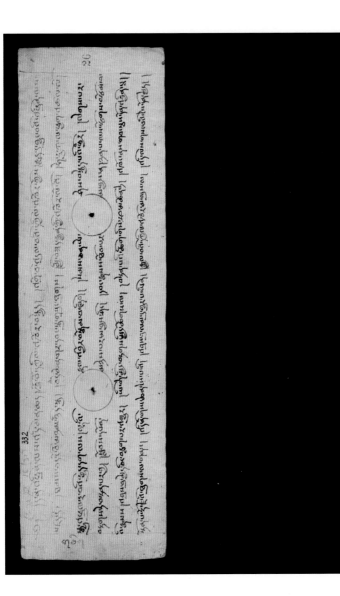

IOL Tib J 332, fol. 1b, 2a ©The British Library

敦煌出土『忿怒五十八尊儀軌』

田中公明

A Ritual Manual
of the Fifty-eight Wrathful Deities
from Dunhuang

Introduction, Tibetan Text and Related Studies

Kimiaki TANAKA

渡辺出版 2020
WATANABE PUBLISHING Co., Ltd., Tokyo 2020.

忿怒五十八尊曼荼羅(富山県南砺市利賀村「瞑想の郷」)

Maṇḍala of the Fifty-eight Wrathful Deities

(Toga Meditation Museum, Toyama Prefecture, JAPAN)

目次（Contents）

ヴィマラミトラ

Vimalamitra

(From *Deities and Divinities of Tibet*)

Summary in Tibetan

སྤྱི་ལོ་ ༡༠༠ ཚམ་ལ་ཏུན་ཧོང་ཕྲུག་ཁུག་ནས་ཐོན་པའི་གནའ་བོའི་བོད་ཡིག་དཔེ་ཆ་
རྣམས་ཀྱི་ཁྲོད་དུ་བོད་བཙན་པོའི་དུས་སྐབས་ཀྱི་ནང་པ་སངས་རྒྱས་པའི་ལུགས་ཀྱི་
གསང་སྔགས་རྡོ་རྗེ་ཐེག་པའི་གཞུང་གལ་གནད་ཆེ་བ་མང་ཚམ་བཞུགས་ཡོད་པ་
དེ་དག་ལས། ཉོང་ལོན་ཌན་(London)དུ་ཡིན་དཔེ་མཛོད་ཁང་(British Library)
དུ་བཞུགས་པའི་ཚོས་ཚན་ IOL Tib J 332 ནི་དེང་གི་བོད་བརྒྱུད་ནང་བསྟན་རྙིང་
མའི་ཚོས་བརྒྱུད་ཀྱི་ཕྱག་བཞེས་སུ་ཡོད་པའི་ཁྲོ་བོ་ལྷ་བཅུ་ང་བརྒྱུད་ཀྱི་ཚོག་ཞིག་ཡིན་
པར་སྣང་།

འདིར་ཏུན་ཧོང་མ་དཔེའི་ཚོ་ག་དེ་ཉིད་དུ་དུངས་པའི་རྒྱུད་ཆེན་གསང་བའི་སྙིང་པོ་ལ་
སོགས་པ་དང་བསྟུན་ནས་ཞུས་སྒྲིག་བགྱིས་ཏེ་གཏན་ལ་ཕབས་པ་ཡིན་ནོ།། ཚོན་ཀྱང་
བདུ་རྗིང་སོགས་དག་ཆ་འི་སྤྱོ་རྗེང་གྲས་འགའ་རེ་མ་བཅོས་པར་མ་དཔེ་སོར་བཞག
བྱས་ཡོད། དེ་ཚམ་མ་ཟད་ཚོ་ག་འདིའི་མཛན་ཏོགས་ཀྱི་རིམ་པ་རྣམས་མཉེན་ཏོགས་
པདེ་བའི་ཆེད་ཡང་གྲངས་ ༡ ནས་ ༣༠ བར་གྱིས་བཅད་བཀོད་ནས་པར་སྐྲུན་བྱས་
ཡོད། ཞིབ་ཕྲ་མཉེན་པར་འདོད་ན་དཔེ་ཆ་འདིའི་ནང་ལ་ཡོད་པའི་དབྱིན་སྐད་ཀྱི་
འགྲེལ་བཤད་ (introduction) ལ་གཟིགས་རོགས་གནང་།།

སྤྱི་ལོ་ ༢༠༡༠ ཟླ་ ༡༡ ཚེས་ ༢༠ ལ་ཞུས་སྒྲིག་པས་བྲིས།།

5

忿怒五十八尊曼荼羅　配置図

（富山県南砺市利賀村「瞑想の郷」）

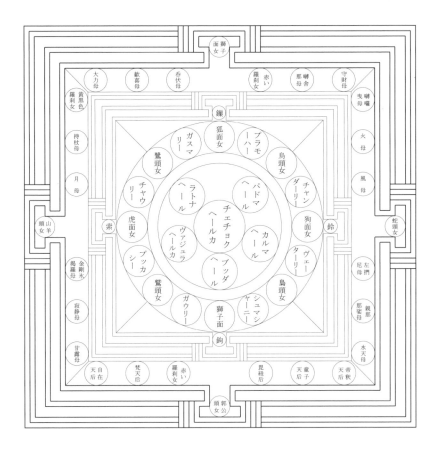

The Maṇḍala of the Fifty-eight Wrathful Deities

(Toga Meditation Museum)

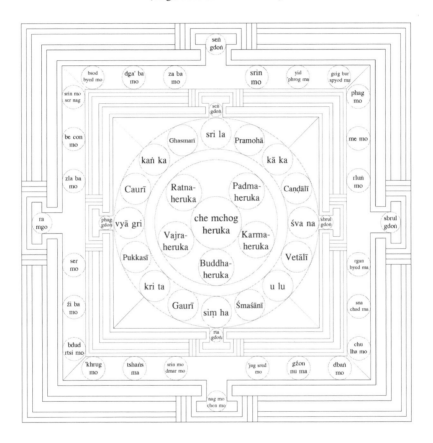

A Ritual Manual of the Fifty-eight Wrathful Deities

文 献 概 説

[1]はじめに

　すでに拙著『敦煌　密教と美術』（法藏館）で紹介したように、敦煌莫高
窟の蔵経洞からは、多数のチベット語密教文献が出土している。その中でも、
今日のニンマ派の密教図像の基礎である寂静忿怒百尊を、寂静四十二尊とと
もに構成する忿怒五十八尊の儀軌は、今日のチベット仏教ニンマ派の前身で
ある吐蕃時代の古密教を解明する上で、かけがえのない資料である。それら
は吐蕃占領期の敦煌密教ばかりでなく、ニンマ派の前身である吐蕃の古密教
を考える上でも、その重要性ははかり知れない。

　本書では、これら忿怒五十八尊の儀軌の解読を通して、吐蕃占領期の敦煌
におけるチベット古密教の一端を紹介してみたい。

[2]忿怒五十八尊とは何か？

　それではまず、本書の中心的テーマである忿怒五十八尊について、簡単に
見ることにしたい。寂静忿怒百尊Źi khro brgya tham baは、チベット仏教ニ
ンマ派に伝承される一連の尊格群で、寂静四十二尊（シ）と忿怒五十八尊（ト）
の二群で合計が百尊よりなるため、寂静忿怒（シト）百尊と呼ばれる。

　ニンマ派は、吐蕃王国時代（仏教前伝期）に伝えられた古密教を中心に、若
干の民俗的要素が加わって成立した宗派である。吐蕃王国では、インドで盛
んになりつつあった後期密教の反社会性を警戒し、その摂取に慎重な姿勢を
とっていた。しかしパドマサンバヴァ、ヴィマラミトラVimalamitra、ヴァイ
ローチャナVairocanaらによって伝えられた密教は、民間に根をおろし、吐蕃
解体後もチベット仏教の底辺を形成するようになった。

　寂静忿怒百尊は、ニンマ派に伝えられるマハーヨーガ乗の仏説部bka' maの

8

「タントラ部」に属する『マーヤージャーラ』（幻化網）十八大部に説かれる諸尊を取捨選択し、百尊にまとめたものと考えられる。またこの寂静忿怒尊の儀軌の一つ『シト・ゴンパランドル』が、E.ヴェンツによって『チベット死者の書』として英訳されたため、欧米では『チベット死者の書』の曼荼羅として知られるようになった。

　その作例は、寂静・忿怒で二幅一対のタンカとするものもあるが、二面一対の壁画として描かれることも多い。

　これに対して敦煌では、寂静四十二尊と忿怒五十八尊関係の写本は、別個に発見されている。この事実は、敦煌文献の時代には、この二つの体系は、いまだ一つに統合されていなかったことを示唆している。

　すでに筆者が他稿で論じたように、寂静四十二尊は『秘密集会タントラ』と『初会金剛頂経』の尊格群を合成して成立したと考えられる。これに対して忿怒五十八尊は、『サマーヨーガ・タントラ』と『初会金剛頂経』「降三世品」の尊格群を合成してつくられている。

　ニンマ派の伝統では、『秘密集会』と『サマーヨーガ』は、ともにマハーヨーガ乗の十八大部(sDe pa bco brgyad)に含まれている。したがって、これらのタントラは、後期密教の中では最初期に属し、吐蕃への仏教伝播の時代には、すでに成立していたと考えられるのである。

　なお本書では参考のため、表紙カヴァーに、著者が主任学芸員を務める富山県南砺市利賀村「瞑想の郷」所蔵の忿怒五十八尊曼荼羅の写真を用い、6頁には、その配置図を掲載した。適宜参照されたい。

[3] 文献の概観
　現在までに同定された忿怒五十八尊関係の写本は、大英図書館所蔵のIOL

Tib J 332と716、フランス国立図書館所蔵Pelliot No.321の３文献である。

　このうちIOL Tib J 716は、漢文の巻子本経典の紙背に、乱雑なチベット語のウメー体で書写されている。内容から見てIからⅢまでの３文献に分割できるが、[1]このうちIは後期密教的な「菩提心」の観法を説き、忿怒五十八尊とは直接関係がない。これに対してⅡは、忿怒五十八尊の中心をなすヘールカと妃の忿怒自在母Krodheśvarī、ガウリー等の８女尊、そして鳥獣の頭をもつタメンマphra men maと呼ばれる８女尊の、合計18尊のみを説いている。そしてその冒頭部分には、「大吉祥なるシュリーヘールカを羯磨の尊格として成就する方便においては」dPal chen po śri he ru ka las kyi lhar bskyur(*sic*) ba'i thabs laとあるので、これを本文献の題名とすべきであろう。

　いっぽうこれに連続するⅢも、忿怒女尊の出生を説く儀軌であるが、現行の忿怒五十八尊とは異なる尊格群が登場するので、別文献と考えた方がよい。

　いっぽうPelliot No.321は、ウチェン文字で記されたペチャ形の写本で、現状では24葉と、現在までに同定された忿怒五十八尊の儀軌としては、分量が最も多い。その内容も、調伏法の意義について述べるなど興味深い点があるが、写本は24bで途絶しており、これに接続する断片はいまだ発見されていない。

　これに対してIOL Tib J 332は、22葉よりなるペチャ形の写本で、巻頭から末尾まで一葉の欠落もない完本であるばかりでなく、IOL Tib J 716に比すと、かなりしっかりしたウメー体で記されている。また一部に、筆記者のミスで記述が欠落した箇所が認められるが、今日のニンマ派が伝えるものとほぼ同じ忿怒五十八尊の図像と観想法が記されており、吐蕃期の古密教の実態を知る上で、貴重な資料といえる。

　なおこの他にも、ヘールカやダーキニーに言及する多数のチベット語断片が存在するが、現在のところ『初会金剛頂経』「降三世品」系、『サマーヨー

ガ』系、チベット古密教系のいずれに属するのか明確でない。

　そこで本書では、現在のところ唯一の完本であるIOL Tib J 332の次第にしたがい、IOL Tib J 716やPelliot No.321にもパラレルな部分が存在する場合は適宜参照しながら、吐蕃時代の古密教における忿怒五十八尊信仰の実態を見てゆきたい。

[4] IOL Tib J 332の内容

　それでは写本の内容を概観してみよう。なお写本の文字は、現在のチベット語正書法の上からは誤った綴字も、一々注記せずそのまま転写している。なおkha'と記したのは、kha字のつぎに'a字が現れる場合のみであり、kha字の下に小さく'a字が書かれる場合はkh'aと転写している。

(1)序

　まずヘールカに帰敬した後、「『マーヤージャーラ』(幻網)等のタントラにより、本尊瑜伽lha'i rnal 'byorを修する者は、衆生に智を生ぜしめるために、よく分別して説くべきである」という。現在でもニンマ派では、寂静忿怒百尊の教法は、「内の三乗」のうちマハーヨーガ乗の『マーヤージャーラ』系であるとするが、このような解釈が、吐蕃の古密教以来のものであることが確認できる。

　そして「阿闍梨を喜ばせず、灌頂等を受けず、聴聞[のみ]に励む者は、果が無く徒労におわるであろう」と戒めるが、これはニンマ派が伝える古タントラの一つで、マハーヨーガ乗の『マーヤージャーラ』系を要約したとされる『サンワイニンポ』に、同一偈が存在することがわかった。[2]。また「これこそ了義の大秘密であり、果を道とするものである。総ての勝者の曼荼羅において、これより秘密の了義はない」と、この教法の優越性が示されるが、

これも前述の『サンワイニンポ』からの引用であることがわかった。[3]

そして酔象の如き心を鎮めるため、寂静処に赴き、禅定を修して煩悩を浄め、三界を調伏し、大我慢を生ぜんがため、「幻網」の三昧を修するという。

(2)平等性の三摩地

つぎに1b5から6にかけて、「以上で忿怒の曼荼羅の成就法no pyi ka[4]が終了したら、まず平等性の三摩地を修習すべし」とあり、一切法は本来生滅を離れており、どのような神変が出現しても、勝義においては、生滅なき界dbyiṅsより微塵も離れることはないと想う。

そして「それは何を意味しているかといえば、その大タントラに、このように説かれている」とあって偈を引用するが、これも前述の『サンワイニンポ』に、同一偈が存在することがわかった。[5]

このように本文献では、散文で次第を略述した後、偈によって同一の内容を再説する場合が多い。そしてこれから見るように、それらの多くは『サンワイニンポ』などの古タントラに、同一あるいは類似偈が存在することがわかった。

(3)日輪観

つぎに「いまや普明大慈の三摩地kun du snaṅ sñiṅ rje chen po'i tiṅ ṅe 'dzin[6]を修すべきであり」とあり、Ma字より日輪が生じ、虚空界を赤く照らすと観想する。忿怒尊を生起する前段階としての日輪観は、敦煌出土のチベット語密教文献『金剛吽迦羅成就法』[7]にも見られたが、本儀軌では日輪上に観想された金剛杵から主尊ブッダ・ヘールカを生起しており、後期密教系の五相成身観における日輪観導入の先駆をなすものとして注目される。

(4)金剛杵の観想

つぎに赤褐色のHuṃ字により、日輪の中心に金剛杵を観想する。そして hum spha ra na Jaḥの真言により光線が十方に放たれて衆生を利益し、saṅ ha ra na Huṅの真言により再び収束し、前のHuṅ字に溶融すると観想する。そしてva jra ti sta ti sta(*sic*)の真言により、五鈷金剛杵となると観想する。

(5)ブッダ・ヘールカの出生

つぎにOṃ 'bu ta śi ri he ru ka huṃの真言により、自身がブッダ・ヘールカとなると観想する。ブッダ・ヘールカはnavarasa[8)]を具すが、勝義においては寂静śāntaなる法性身chos ñid kyi skuから動かないとの記述があり、注目される。

(6)氈毛の界とカパーラの楼閣

つぎにra rag ta ra rag taの真言により、よく磨きあげられた紅珊瑚のような紅色のra字から、宇宙大の血液の氈毛の界lva kloṅを生起する。それは東の氈毛が南、南が西、西が北に渦巻いている。つぎにBa Baの真言により、カパーラban 'daでできた曼荼羅の楼閣を観想する。その構造は、外と内がなく、十方の総てを包含している。このように楼閣は、血液の氈毛界の中心に、脊椎を須弥山とし、上には智慧の火焔が燃え熾るなかに観想される。

(7)四輻輪の観想と讃

つぎに'Bruṅ byi śva byi śud deの真言により、大火焔をともなう四輻輪に、四角にして四門、二重の走廊を有し、カパーラ、蛇、日月、新古の屍体などによって飾られた曼荼羅の楼閣を観想する。なお二重の走廊とあるのは、この曼荼羅が、五部ヘールカ等の仏教内部の尊格を内院、ヒンドゥー教から取

り入れられた二十八ワンチュクマを外院に配する二重構造をとるためと思われる。

さらに輪の四輻には、それぞれ乾闥婆(東)、夜叉(南)、羅刹(西)、閻魔(北)の男女が居り、それらを牛王(東)、灰黒色の有翼水牛(南)、豹(西)、虎(北)が爪で捉えると規定されている。因みにこの配置も、『サンワイニンポ』に典拠がある。

敦煌からは、ギメ美術館所蔵のEO.3579のように、曼荼羅の四門に動物を描いた作品や、拙著『敦煌 密教と美術』第9章で取りあげた「八大明王儀軌」のように、曼荼羅の四門に動物を配することを規定した文献が出土している。これらの配置は、本文献の所説と完全には一致しないが、四門に鳥獣を配する意匠は、チベット系古密教の影響ではないかと思われる。

また偈によって、四輻輪と曼荼羅の観想を再説するが、これも『サンワイニンポ』からの引用であることがわかった。[9]

(8)忿怒自在母の出生

つぎに自らは一切如来身口意金剛の自性である忿怒王となり、Hi Hiと唱えることにより、その左側に妃の忿怒自在母Kro ti śva riを観想する。忿怒自在母の尊容は、主尊(ブッダ・ヘールカ)とほぼ同じであるが、頭冠はない。そして'Ja Huṃ Paṅ Hoの四明により、鉤召、引入、鏁縛、歓喜せしめ、菩提心が妃の虚空mkh'aつまり女性器に落ちると想う。

そして出生偈を唱えた後、Huṃ Huṃ byi śva gro ti jva la man 'da la phat phat ha la ha laと唱えて、男女尊から生じた菩提心から光が放たれ、十方の六道の世界が、種々の器杖を持った忿怒尊で満たされると観想する。なおこの部分も、『サンワイニンポ』にほぼパラレルな一節がある。[10]

(9)四部ヘールカと婆伽梵大楽の出生

つぎにこの中から、東方ヴァジュラ・ヘールカ、南方ラトナ・ヘールカ、西方パドマ・ヘールカ、北方カルマ・ヘールカが無数に出生すると観想する。

そして婆伽梵大楽dgyes chen poが、大千世界の微塵に等しい手に世界の微塵に等しい器杖を持ち、大千世界の微塵に等しい足は、展右brkyaṅ skumの勢で大自在天夫妻等を踏みつけると観想する。

そしてこれらの忿怒尊は、大怖畏の姿をし、大叫喚をあげ、劫火の燃えさかる中に、三面六臂四足の姿になって、それぞれ乾闥婆(東)夜叉(南)羅刹(西)閻魔(北)の男女一対の台座の上に展右の勢で立つと観想する。なおここでは、忿怒尊はすべて三面六臂四足と規定され、婆伽梵大楽は無数の手足を持つとした先の記述と矛盾する。したがって三面六臂四足とは、大楽尊ではなく、四方に出生した四部ヘールカについての規定と考えられる。

なお現在のチベット仏教ニンマ派では、忿怒五十八尊全体を一身に集約した忿怒尊チェチョク・ヘールカが説かれるが、その尊容は、ここで説かれる婆伽梵大楽尊に類似している。おそらく現在のチェチョク・ヘールカは、このような婆伽梵大楽尊に起源を有するものであろう。

そして東方に出生した無数のヘールカは、ヴァジュラ・ヘールカ一尊に集約され、南西北の三方に出生したヘールカも、それぞれラトナ・ヘールカ、パドマ・ヘールカ、カルマ・ヘールカ一尊となり、四方に座を占めると観想する。

(10)四忿怒自在母の出生

つづいてgro ti śva ri 'Ja Huṃ Pam Hoと唱えて、主尊の左側に妃の忿怒自在母Krodheśvarīを観想する。現在の忿怒五十八尊では、四部ヘールカと忿怒自在母は、新訳派の父母仏と同様に、男女尊が正対して抱擁しているが、こ

の儀軌では、男性尊の左側に女性尊を観想するように説いている。これは拙著『敦煌　密教と美術』第6章で取り上げた敦煌出土の寂静四十二尊曼荼羅と同じ形態であり、敦煌文献の時代には、男女尊が正対する父母仏は、いまだ成立していなかったか、少なくとも一般的ではなかったことが裏づけられる。

(11)ガウリー等の女性尊の出生

　ついで男女尊の不二の菩提心の雲から、Ha Ha Ha Ha Ha Ha Ha Haと唱えることにより、ガウリーdKar mo等の七種の女性尊の集団が出生する。なおこの直後に唱えられる眷属尊出生の偈も、『サンワイニンポ』にパラレルな一節がある。[11]

(12)鳥獣の頭をもつ女性尊の出生

　さらに男女尊の不二の菩提心の雲から、He He He He He He He Heと唱えることにより、獅子面女Seṅ gdoṅ chen mo等の九種の女性尊の集団が出生する。なおこの直後に唱えられる鳥獣の頭をした女性尊出生の偈も、『サンワイニンポ』にほぼパラレルな一節を見出すことができる。[12]

(13)門衛の出生

　さらに男女尊の不二の菩提心の雲から、Phaṭ Phaṭ Phaṭ Phaṭと唱えることにより、金剛長行女rDo rje bsriṅs 'gro ma等の四種の門衛の集団が出生する。この直後に唱えられる偈は、『サンワイニンポ』には見出すことができないが、(12)の鳥獣の頭をもつ女性尊の出生を説いた直後に、ほぼ同様の次第が説かれている。[13]

(14)忿怒尊群の出生

　さらに男女尊の不二の菩提心の雲から、Phatと唱えることにより、忿怒の形相著しい忿怒尊の雲霞の如き集団が、すべて出生すると想う。

(15)任運成就観

　つぎに任運成就lhun gyis grub paをなすべきであるという。その次第は、男女尊の不二の菩提心から智慧の光明が生じ、自身の身口意の三業を浄める。菩提心が熱せられた黄金のようになり、Oṃ Āḥ Hūṃと唱えることにより、これら三字の文字鬘が連なって自身の心臓に溶融する。そしてさらに心臓から金剛道rdo rje lamつまり尿道を通って、妃の虚空mkha(女性器)に溶融し、法性は菩提心の自性となり、その界dbyiṅsから、諸尊の真言と心真言などが出生すると観想する。

　この次第は、著者が先に紹介した『秘密集会』「ジュニャーナパーダ流」の生起次第の観想法[14]に類似している。

(16)空智金剛・四智・三金剛・随愛・供養の真言

　つづいて空智金剛、大円鏡智、妙観察智、平等性智、成所作智、身金剛加持、口金剛加持、意金剛加持、随愛金剛、供養金剛の真言と語句の訳が説かれる。このうち妙観察智と平等性智は、通常と順序が逆転しているが、本文献では妙観察智の真言を平等性智mñam ba ñid kyi ye śes chen po、平等性智の真言を妙観察察so so kun du rtog pa'i ye śes chen poと訳しており、両者を取り違えていることがわかる。なおこれら一連の真言は、『サンワイニンポ』に同一の順序で見出すことができる。[15]このうち空智金剛の真言は『秘密集会タントラ』「第三分」[16]、身口意三金剛加持と随愛、供養の真言は『秘密集会』「第六分」に説かれるが、[17]四智の真言は、ニンマ派のタントラ以外

A Ritual Manual of the Fifty-eight Wrathful Deities

には見出すことが難しい。

(17)四支

8a5に「ここまでは、勝者の子として自身を生起するのである。このように五智の自性と我慢を生起した後、いまやこれ以後は、自己の子として勝者を生起すべきなのである」とあって、この前後で、観想の質が変化することがわかる。

これは『秘密集会』「ジュニャーナパーダ流」において、「識」支に相当する次第で、普賢父母仏から「因の持金剛」が生まれるた後、「生」支に相当する次第では「因の持金剛」から眷属尊が生まれることを想起させる。

そしてこれ以後は、(6)から(14)までで説かれた曼荼羅の楼閣と諸尊の出生のプロセスが、(18)から(27)までの次第においては、真言による生起という方法で追体験されることになる。

さらに男性尊の五鈷金剛杵(男性器)の先端に一字を修し、妃の虚空(女性器)の八葉蓮華上に、Ma字より日輪を観想する。つづいて'Dz'a Hūṃ Paṃ H'oの四明により、男性尊の標幟を鉤召、引入、鑽縛し、歓喜せしめ、菩提心を妃の虚空に[放出したと]観想する。

さらに妃の秘密の四処を、親近の四支bsñen pa'i yan lag bźiによって安立すべきであるとして、『サンワイニンポ』より偈を引用する。なお親近の四支とは、『秘密集会タントラ』所説の親近・近成就・成就・大成就の四支を意味するが、本文献は、その具体的内容までは説いていない。

(18)曼荼羅の生起

そして'Bruṃ vyi śva vyi śud deと唱えることにより、秘密の曼荼羅を生じる。その曼荼羅は、(6)において生起した血液の氈毛の界と、脊椎の須弥山と、

カパーラの楼閣などの、おどろおどろしい装飾を備えている。

(19)ブッダ・ヘールカの生起

　そしてOṃ 'bu da śri he ru ka ma ha tsan ta sa rva dus stan da ka ha na pa tsa Hūṃ Phatと唱えて、曼荼羅の中心にブッダ・ヘールカを生起する。その尊容は身色煙黒色、三面六臂で、魔女bdud maとルドラの夫妻を踏みつける。また六臂には、右の第一手に鉄囲山を伴う千世界、第二手に金剛杵、第三手に智慧の鍬、左の第一手は斧鉞、第二手に剣、第三手に智慧の鍬を持ち、主尊と同じ姿をした妃の忿怒自在母を左側に伴なう。

(20)ヴァジュラ・ヘールカの生起

　つぎにOṃ va jra ma ha śri he ru k'a sa rva dus stan da ka ha na pa tsa Hūṃ Phat/ Oṃ dar ma kro ti śva ri Hūṅ Phatと唱えて、曼荼羅の東の輻にヴァジュラ・ヘールカを生起する。その尊容は身色青黒色、三面六臂で、ガンダルヴァ夫妻を大鵬の爪で捕捉している。また六臂はブッダ・ヘールカと同じく、右の第一手に鉄囲山を伴う千世界、第二手に金剛杵、第三手に智慧の鍬、左の第一手は斧鉞、第二手に剣、第三手に智慧の鍬を持ち、主尊と同じ姿をした妃の(ヴァジュラ・)クローデーシュヴァリーを左側に伴なう。

(21)ラトナ・ヘールカの生起

　つぎにOṃ rad na ma ha śri he ru ka ma ha can dha sa rva du śtan da ka ha na pa tsa Hūṃ Phat/ Oṃ su rya rad na kro ti śva ri Hūṃ Phatと唱えて、曼荼羅の南の輻にラトナ・ヘールカを生起する。その尊容は身色黄黒色、三面六臂で、夜叉夫妻を有翼水牛の爪で捕捉している。また六臂は、右の第一手に鉄囲山を伴う千世界、第二手に金剛杵、第三手に血を盛ったカパーラ、左の第

一手は斧鉞、第二手に剣、第三手に智慧の鍬を持ち、主尊と同じ姿をした妃のラトナ・クローデーシュヴァリーを左側に伴なう。

(22)パドマ・ヘールカの生起

つぎにOṃ pad ma śri he ru ga ma ha tsan da sa rva du stan da ka ha na pa tsa Hūṃ Phat/ Oṃ hri śa ta pa ka ma/ ma ha kro ti śva ri byi śa byi śud de Hūṃ Phatと唱えて、曼荼羅の西の輻にパドマ・ヘールカを生起する。その尊容は身色赤黒色、三面六臂で、羅刹夫妻を豹の爪で捕捉している。また六臂は、右の第一手に鉄囲山を伴う千世界、第二手に金剛杵、第三手に血を盛ったカパーラ、左の第一手は斧鉞、第二手に剣、第三手に智慧の鍬を持ち、主尊と同じ姿をした妃のパドマ・クローデーシュヴァリーを左側に伴なう。

(23)カルマ・ヘールカの生起

つぎにOṃ kar ma ma ha śri he ru ka ma ha tsan da sa rva du śtan da ka ha na pa tsa Hūṃ Phat/ Oṃ ma ha a mo ka Hūṃ Phatと唱えて、曼荼羅の北の輻にカルマ・ヘールカを生起する。その尊容は身色緑黒色、三面六臂で、焔魔夫妻を虎の爪で捕捉している。また六臂は、右の第一手に鉄囲山を伴う千世界、第二手に金剛杵、第三手に血を盛ったカパーラ、左の第一手は斧鉞、第二手に剣、第三手に智慧の鍬を持ち、主尊と同じ姿をした妃のカルマ・クローデーシュヴァリーを左側に伴なう。

(24)ガウリー等の8女尊の生起

つぎにva jra ge'u ri haと唱えて、曼荼羅の外側の東の屍体の上に、ガウリ

(表1)ガウリー等八女尊の図像

尊名	方位	IOL Tib J 332			IOL Tib J 716			Pelliot No.321		
		身色	右手	左手	色	右手	左手	色	右手	左手
ガウリー	東	青	屍の杖	盛血劫波杯	青	屍の杖	盛血劫波杯	青	屍の杖	盛血劫波杯
チャウリー	南	黄	弓矢をつがえる		黄	矢をつがえる		黄	弓矢をつがえる	
プラモーハー	西	赤	摩竭幢を持つ		赤	摩竭幢を持つ		赤	左に摩竭幢を持つ	
ヴェーターリー	北	黒	右は金剛杵を振り回し、左は死体の腰部を攫んで食する		黒	金剛杵	死体を攫り食する	黒	金剛杵	死体を攫り食する
プッカシー	東南	赤黄	右は死体の頭を押さえ、左は死体の腸脂を引き出して食する		記載が欠落			赤黄	死体からvasutaを引き出して服用する	
ガスマリー	南西	緑	左は盛血劫波杯を持ち、右手の九鈷杵で服用する		判読困難			緑	攪拌して服用する	盛血劫波杯
シュマシャーニー	西北	濃青	右は死体の足を握り、左は頭を攫み、歯で死体から心臓を引き出す		記載が欠落			青	両手で死体の頭と尾をつかむ	
チャンダーリー	北東	淡黄	左で死体の腰部を攫み、頭蓋骨を切断して主尊に奉献する		記載が欠落			赤	劫波杯を持つ	死体をつかむ

ーを生起する。その尊容は身色青色、一面二臂で、右手で屍体の杖を振り上げ、左手は血を盛ったカパーラから[血液を]服用する。以下南、西、北には、チャウリー、プラモーハー、ヴェーターリー、東南、南西、西北、北東の四維には、プッカシー、ガスマリー、シュマシャーニー、チャンダーリーの4女尊が、順次観想される。なおこれらの8女尊は最初期の母タントラ『サマーヨーガ』に現れるが、sme śa canは梵名をシュマシャーニーとするものとドーンビーとするものがあり、どちらが正しいか不明であった。ところが本文献は、当該尊の真言を『サンワイニンポ』と同じくva jra sma śa niとしており、シュマシャーニーの可能性を示唆している。

　なおガウリー等の8女尊については、IOL Tib J 716やPelliot No.321にも尊容が記述されている。残念ながらIOL Tib J 716は、筆記者のミスにより、東南のガスマリーの後、鳥獣の頭をもつ8女尊の西南に配される鷺頭女まで記述が飛んでおり、一部の尊容しか明らかでないが、3者を対照して表1に示した。なおガウリー等の尊容に関しては、3文献の記述はほぼ一致し、現在

(表2)鳥獣の頭をもった八女尊の図像

尊名	IOL Tib J 332				IOL Tib J 716			Pelliot No.321		
	方位	身色	右手	左手	色	右手	左手	色	右手	左手
獅子面女	東		記載が欠落		記載が欠落			黄	両手の金剛拳を肩頭で交え、死体を噛む	
虎面女	南	赤	両手の印を肩頭で交え歯で死体から心臓を引き出す		記載が欠落			赤	両手を交え、腐乱した死体を?する。	
狐面女	西	黒	両手で死体の皮を剥ぎ、全人皮の敷物とする		記載が欠落			黒	両手で死体を引き裂き、舌で咀嚼する	
狗面女	北	青黒	右足で死体の頭、左足で足を踏みつけ、両手で腸脂と内臓を食する		記載が欠落			黒	両手で死体を握り破壊する	
鷲頭女	東南	赤	盛血劫波杯	剃刀を持つ	記載が欠落			赤黒	刀を持つ	盛血劫波杯
鷺頭女	南西	黄	両手で死体の皮を剥ぎ、両足を巻き付けて、肩で交える。		白赤	死体を左肩に背負う		白赤	刀	死体を肩に背負う
烏頭女	西北	黒	盛血劫波杯	剃刀を持つ	黒	蓮華器	曲刀	黒	刀	盛血劫波杯
梟頭女	北東	栗色	盛血劫波杯	金剛鉤で鉤召する	雑色	盛血螺貝	金剛鉤	緑	鉤を持つ	盛血劫波杯

のニンマ派の流布図像とも大きな差違は見られない。したがってガウリー等の8女尊の図像は、吐蕃時代には、ほぼ定まっていたと思われる。

(25)獅子面女等の鳥獣の頭をもつ8女尊の生起

　そのさらに外側には、獅子面女等の鳥獣の頭をもつ8女尊を生起するが、写本に欠落があり、獅子面女の尊容は明確に説かれていない。つぎの虎面女は、身色赤色、一面二臂で虎の頭をもち、印を結んだ手を肩先で交差させ、屍体の心臓を歯で引き出して服用?している。以下西と北には、狐面女と狗面女、東南、南西、西北、北東の四維には、鷲頭女、鷺頭女、烏頭女、梟頭女の4女尊が順次観想される。なおこれらの8女尊の尊名も、現在の忿怒五十八尊と一致している。

　いっぽうIOL Tib J 716には、鷲頭女以下の３尊のみ尊容が記述されている。これにPelliot No.321を加えた三者を対照して、表２に示した。なお鳥獣の頭をもつ８女尊に関しては、二つの文献の記述と現在のニンマ派の流布図像の間に、かなりの差違が見られる。また鷲頭女以下の４尊では、IOL Tib J 332, 716とPelliot No.321の間で、左右手の持物が逆転している。これは尊格の左右の手と、絵画での向かって左右の手を取り違えた可能性があり、儀軌の作者が当時敦煌にあった何らかの図像を参照したことを示唆している。

(表３)門衛の四女尊の図像

	IOL Tib J 332				Pelliot No. 321			
	門	身色	右手	左手	門	身色	右手	左手
馬頭鉤女	東	白	鉤	剃刀	東	青褐	鉤	盛血劫波杯
猪頭索女	南	青	索	猪の牙を露出	南	青黒	猪の牙	盛血劫波杯
日月目女	西	赤	金剛杵	鉤(鏃の誤り？)	西	赤黒	金剛鏃	盛血劫波杯
灰鈴女	北	緑	金剛鈴	金剛鉤	北	？	金剛鈴を鳴らす	盛血劫波杯

(26)門衛の四女尊の生起

　その外側の東門には、馬頭鉤女rta gdoṅ lcags kyu maを生起する。馬頭鉤女は、身色白色、右手には鉤、左手には剃刀を持つ。以下南西北の三門には、それぞれ猪頭索女、日月目女、灰鈴女の４女尊が、順次観想される。なおこれらの門衛の４女尊の尊名も『サマーヨーガ』に現れるが、北門の thal byed は、梵名が明らかでなかった。ところが本文献は、当該尊の真言を『サンワイニンポ』と同じくva jra pa smyi ba la te ho、Pelliot No.321でもva jra pa smyi pa la ya hoとしており、Vajrabhasmī(金剛灰女)の可能性を示唆している。[18]

　なおこれらの４女尊については、IOL Tib J 716には記述がないので、

Pelliot No.321のみと対照して表３に示した。

(27)二十八ワンチュクマの生起

　そのさらに外側には、Bhyoの真言により28尊のワンチュクマを生起する。ワンチュクマの配置は、四方に６尊、四門に各１尊で、現在のニンマ派の忿怒五十八尊にほぼ一致する。なお現在のワンチュクマは全員が鳥獣の頭をもっているが、IOL Tib J 332では、西側の第三Grub moが狐面、北側の第六水天母Chu'i lha moがマカラの頭、南門のRa mgo maが山羊頭をもつことを除いては、鳥獣の頭に関する記述がない。また東側の第二梵天后'Tsaṅs maでは、ヒンドゥー教の梵天と同じ四面が規定されており、他のワンチュクマは、人間の頭をもっていたと思われる。

　著者が他書で論じたように、二十八ワンチュクマは『初会金剛頂経』「降三世品」に説かれる二十天后を増広して構成されている。(69頁表参照)[19]しかし『初会金剛頂経』の二十天后は、原則として人間の頭をもつ天女として表現されており、[20]全員が鳥獣の頭をもつワンチュクマは、敦煌文献の時代には、いまだ成立していなかったのではないかと思われる。いっぽうPelliot No.321は、非常に浩瀚な儀軌であるにもかかわらず、現存部分には二十八ワンチュクマの尊容を詳述した箇所が見あたらない。

　そこで二十八ワンチュクマについては、本文献と『サンワイニンポ』そして『初会金剛頂経』「降三世品」所説の二十天后を対照させ、69頁の表に示した。なおIOL Tib J 332の説くワンチュクマの名称と配置は、現行の埋蔵系の儀軌より『サンワイニンポ』に近い。しかし『サンワイニンポ』が詳説しないワンチュクマの身色や持物において、本文献の記述の一部が、現行の儀軌に一致することもわかった。

　これは本文献が、後期密教における母天受容の初期の段階から、現行の忿

怒五十八尊への移行過程にあることを暗示している。

(28)曼荼羅の鉤召

　そして「それは何をあらわしているかといえば、そのタントラ自体より、このように説くべきである」とあって、『サンワイニンポ』を引用して、[21]曼荼羅の殊勝な特相を説く。さらに曼荼羅の諸尊を鉤召する真言Oṃ ru lu ru lu ru lu huṅ bhyo va jra sa ma ya ho// va jra sa ma ya stvam/ va jra sa ma ya ho//が説かれる。

　つづいて「いまやこの成就歌をとる」とあり、忿怒尊の讃と真言Oṃ sa ma ya Oṃ//va jra sa ma ya phaṭ/Ram ā li u li ta li ta pa to śa/ śam mgo na ru ti kha ram yo gi ni Huṅ Hā He Phaṭが説かれる。なおこの成就歌も『サンワイニンポ』に対応する部分がある。[22]

(29)曼荼羅の出現

　そして「このように曼荼羅を明瞭に配置して、十方の六道を完全に覆い尽くす火焔の曼荼羅が明瞭に出現する」とあって、曼荼羅の主尊ヘールカの尊容が、偈によって説かれる。なおこの偈も『サンワイニンポ』からの引用であることがわかった。[23]

　つづいて「支分を完具し、資具を備え、儀軌を遍知し、瑜伽を積集した曼荼羅は、諸事業の悉地を円満せり」と再び『サンワイニンポ』を引用した後、[24]「いまやこの成就歌をとるべきである」とあり、忿怒尊の讃を唱える。なおこの成就歌も『サンワイニンポ』からの引用である。[25]

(30)曼荼羅の収束(随滅)

　そして「いまや大火焔の曼荼羅、自身の蘊界処を収束させるべきである」

とあって、曼荼羅の収束が説かれる。その次第は、自身の蘊界処をHūṃ字に収束させ、さらにそのHūṃ字を、毘盧遮那如来あるいは法界清浄智の自性であるHā、宝生如来あるいは平等性智であるṅaつまり空点、阿弥陀如来あるいは妙観察智である'aつまり長母音記号、不空成就如来あるいは成所作智であるźabs skyed(正しくはźabs kyu)、金剛薩埵あるいは大円鏡智であるthig leつまりナーダ点に分解する。また身口意の三密に約すなら、Haは身密の自性、źabs skyedは口密の自性、thig leが意密の自性であるという。

そしてźabs skyedが長母音記号に、長母音記号がHa字本体に、Ha字が空点に、Haとṅaが荘厳点zla tshesに、ṅaはthig leに溶融すると観想する。そしてthig leが法身と無別であると信解して、収束の状態に好きなだけとどまる。

なおこの観法は、後期サンヴァラ系に特徴的な「随滅」(アヌベーダ)と呼ばれる観想法に酷似している。[26]

ちなみに後期サンヴァラ系では、Hūṃ字を、母音記号と子音字本体、字の頭(シローレーカ)、荘厳点(チャンドラビンドゥ)、空点(アヌスヴァーラ)、ナーダ点の六要素に分解するが、本儀軌では、チベット文字に特有の長母音記号を加えるかわりに、字の頭を構成要素に数えていない。

「随滅」は、後期サンヴァラ系の究竟次第に特徴的に見られるので、成立が下ると考えられていたが、本文献の発見により、その起源は、遅くとも九世紀まで上がることがわかった。

そしてこの節の末尾には「南無、真実の妙現の荘厳の修道法na mo de kho na ñid kyi snaṅ ba dam pa rgyan gi bsgom thabsおわる」とあり、本来は独立していた随滅の観法が、忿怒五十八尊の儀軌に編入された可能性を示している。

(31)諸尊の招入

　そして「このように曼荼羅を明瞭に配置して、いまや大怖畏の曼荼羅を鉤召すべし」とあって、『大タントラ』を引用しつつ、曼荼羅の諸尊を招き入れる。

(32)曼荼羅への入住

　つづいてヘールカ、忿怒自在母、内外のダーキニーたちを偈をもって讃えつつ、曼荼羅に堅固に住せんことを願う。

(33)五甘露の奉献

　つづいて五部ヘールカ、五部忿怒自在母、ガウリー等の8女尊、鳥獣の頭をもつ8女尊、門衛の4女尊、内外の金剛アーラリの順に、偈をもって諸尊を讃えつつ、五甘露sman pan tsa a 'bri taを奉献する。

(34)諸尊の三昧耶形

　「五甘露によって供養される前に、火焔の舞踏と印が出現する」とあって、ガウリー等の8女尊、鳥獣の頭をした8女尊、門衛の4女尊の順に、偈をもって諸尊の尊容を略述する。なおこのうちガウリー等の8女尊の身色と標幟を説いた偈は、『古タントラ全集』に収録される『タクトゥン・ドゥーパ』(飲血集会)というタントラに、ほぼ同一偈が現れることがわかった。[27]

(35)懺悔

　「いまや大怖畏の曼荼羅等において、発露懺悔を献ずべし」とあって、偈をもって、修法において行者が犯した過失を懺悔し、許しを乞う。

(36)四大輪の観想

　つづいてRam Ramによって火輪を生起し、煩悩の習気をことごとく焼盡すると想う。つぎに交叉金剛の地輪rgya gram dbaṅ chen=mahīndraの上に？、Yam Yam字によって風輪を生起し、火によって焼かれた灰を悉く吹き飛ばすと想う。さらにKhaṅ Khaṅによって水輪を生起し、風によって除去できなかった余塵を、悉く洗浄すると想う。

　なお四大輪の観想は、敦煌では漢文系の密教文献にも言及されていることが指摘されている。[28]

(37)五仏の種字の布置

　つづいて五道lam rgyud lṅaを飾るためと称して、頭頂にOṃ、耳にHūṃ、鼻にAṃ、臍にSvā、舌にHaを布置する。これらは『秘密集会』系で、毘盧遮那、阿閦、阿弥陀、宝生、不空成就の種字として広く用いられているが、『秘密集会』系では、頭頂あるいは眉間に毘盧遮那、心臓に阿閦、口あるいは喉に阿弥陀、臍に宝生、両足に不空成就を布置するのが通例である。[29]

　本文献の説く偈によれば、これら五仏の種字を五つの殊勝処に布置すれば、不死になるから恐れることはない、識の住する五蘊を、五仏に布施するのであるという。

(38)教誡と結尾

　そして阿闍梨によって偈が唱えられるが、これも『サンワイニンポ』に対応する箇所がある。[30]とくにその末尾の、「本来不生の真如は、幻や顕現や幻影のようであり、性交sbyorや調伏sgrolをすべて行じても、毫も為したことにはならない」という一節では、古密教が行じた悪法として非難された、性交と調伏に対する擁護が見られることは注目に値する。

　そして22b3にはrdzogs sts-hoとあり、本文献の末尾であることがわかるが、

この後も数行に亙って諸尊の灌頂真言などが記されている。

[5] 結　論

　このように敦煌出土のチベット語密教文献IOL　Tib　J　332，716，Pelliot No.321は、吐蕃時代に伝播した古密教の忿怒五十八尊の儀軌と見ることができる。とくにIOL Tib J 332は、今日のニンマ派に伝えられる忿怒五十八尊の儀軌や図像とも比較的よく一致し、『サンワイニンポ』などニンマ派の古タントラからの引用が多数発見されたことも、貴重である。確実な資料に乏しい吐蕃時代の古密教の知る上で、貴重なテキストといえよう。

　著者が他著で論じたように、忿怒五十八尊は、最初期の母タントラである『サマーヨーガ』と『初会金剛頂経』「降三世品」に説かれた母天(二十天后)を合成して構成されているが、[31]本儀軌は、いくつかの点において古様を示し、後期密教における母天受容の初期の段階から、現在の忿怒五十八尊への移行過程にあると推定される。

　また諸尊の出生に関しては、後期密教の特徴である性的な諸尊の生起を説くが、そのプロセスのいくつかは、著者が他稿で紹介した『秘密集会』「ジュニャーナパーダ流」と類似している。これは吐蕃時代のチベットには「ジュニャーナパーダ流」の原初形態が知られていたという、従来からの推定を裏づけるものと思われる。また後期サンヴァラ系に特徴的な「随滅」の観法の原初形態が見られる点も注目に価する。

　したがって本文献は、単にチベット仏教ニンマ派の密教の原初形態を知るだけでなく、インド後期密教の歴史的展開を考える上でも、貴重な資料と思われる。

　そこで本書では巻末に、同文献をチベット語フォントで復刻した。なお写本の文字は、現在のチベット語正書法の上からは誤った綴字も、一々注記せ

ずそのまま転写している。

　今後も著者は、チベット語密教文献の解読を通じて、敦煌における密教の伝播と歴史的変遷に加え、現在のチベット仏教ニンマ派との関係についても、解明してゆきたいと考えている。

註

1)『スタイン蒐集チベット語文献解題目録』第8分冊（東洋文庫、1984年）pp.35-37参照。なお同カタログは、改訂出版に備えて、すでに原稿の大半のパソコン入力を完了しているが、諸般の事情によりいまだ刊行されていない。

2)北京No.455, Vol.10, 5-3-2〜3.なお北京版には異本No.457も収録されており、ほとんどの引用偈を双方に見出すことができるが、以下ではNo.455における対応箇所を示した。

3)北京No.455, Vol.10, 6-3-2〜4.

4)no pyi kaとは、sādhanopāyikāの後半部分nopāyikāが、誤って成就法の意に用いられたものと思われる。

5)北京No.455, Vol.10, 1-4-5〜6.

6)敦煌ではIOL Tib J 436 IやNo.554にも、大瑜伽の三種三摩地の一つとしてkun tu snaṅ gi tiṅ ṅe 'dzinが説かれるが、これと同一かどうかは今後さらに検討しなければならない。

7)拙著『敦煌　密教と美術』（法藏館、2000年）135-149, 230-246参照。

8)インド・チベット密教におけるnavarasaについては、拙稿「『一切佛集會拏吉尼戒網瑜伽』所説「九味」考」（『東方』第5号、1989年）ならびに「『一切佛集會拏吉尼戒網瑜伽』所説「九味」再考」（『印度学仏教学研究』41-1、1992年）を参照。

9)北京No.455, Vol.10, 8-2-4〜6.

10)*ibid.* 6-5-7以下に類似の次第が出る。

11)*ibid.* 7-3-7〜8.

12)*ibid.* 7-4-1〜3.

13)*ibid.* 7-4-3〜5.

14)拙稿「『秘密集会』ジュニャーナパーダ流の生起次第caturaṅgaの新資料－National Archives pra.1697(kha 2)の研究－」(『＜我＞の思想（前田専学博士還暦記念論文集）』春秋社、1991年)、拙著『性と死の密教』(春秋社、1997年) pp.102-109参照。

15)北京No.455, Vol.10, 3-4-8〜5-2.

16)松長有慶『秘密集会タントラ校訂梵本』(東方出版、1978年) p.11.

17)*ibid.* p.17.

18)その後、『サマーヨーガ・タントラ』を広範囲に引用する『行合集灯』*Caryāmelāmelpakapradīpa*のサンスクリット・テキストが刊行され、金剛灰女の梵名は灰滅起尸Bhasmapralayavetālīであることが確認された。

19)拙著『詳解河口慧海コレクション－チベット・ネパール仏教美術－』(佼成出版社、1990年) p.58参照。

20)金剛界二十天后の図像は、アルチ寺大日堂壁画の降三世大曼荼羅の外院の他には、詳細に描いた作品が知られていなかったが、『国立民族学博物館研究報告別冊』18号に正木晃氏撮影のペンコルチューデ仏塔の三世輪大曼荼羅の写真が掲載され、参照できるようになった。この作例でも、二十天后は原則として通常の天女形で描かれている。

21)北京No.455, Vol.10, 4-5-8〜5-1-1.

22)*ibid.* 8-2-1.

23)*ibid.* 8-2-6〜8.

24)*ibid.* 5-4-5.

25)*ibid.* 9-2-8〜3-4.

26)「随滅」については、奥山直司「インド後期密教における自己神化論」（『インド学・密教学研究』法藏館、1993年所収）、拙著『性と死の密教』（春秋社、1997年）pp.140-141参照。

27)*dPal khrag 'thuṅ 'dus pa rtsa ba'i rgyud*（金子No.381）fol.113, 1.1-3.

28)加地哲定「敦煌本密教文献について」（『密教学密教史論集』、1965年所収）

29)「『秘密集会』ジュニャーナパーダ流の新出文献Mañjuvajramukhyākhyānaについて」（高崎直道博士還暦記念論集『インド学仏教学論集』春秋社、1987年）p.420参照。なお加地上掲28)論文によれば、敦煌出土の漢文文献『大乗四無量安心入道法要略』にも、この五字の観想が出るが、その布置箇所は、本文献と『秘密集会』系の何れとも相違している。

30)北京No.455, Vol.10, 5-4-2〜4.

31)拙著『曼荼羅イコノロジー』（平河出版社、19872年〜現在まで改訂8版）pp.243-252参照。なお同書の初版には、寂静忿怒百尊の尊数の数え方に誤りがあった。重版以後を見られたい。

A Ritual Manual of the Fifty-eight Wrathful Deities

Introduction

[1] Preamble

As described in my *Essays on Tantric Buddhism in Dunhuang: Its Art and Text*, many esoteric Buddhist icons and esoteric Buddhist manuscripts written in Tibetan have been discovered in Dunhuang. Of outstanding importance among these are the ritual manuals of the fifty-eight wrathful deities, which together with the forty-two peaceful deities form the one hundred peaceful and wrathful deities and constitute the basis of the icons of the present-day rÑiṅ ma school of Tibetan Buddhism. They provide indispensable material not only for considering esoteric Buddhism in Dunhuang during its Tibetan occupation but also for restoring the old tantric school transmitted at the time of the ancient Tibetan empire (Tufan), which was the predecessor of today's rÑiṅ ma school.

In this monograph, I shall consider the old tantric school in Dunhuang during its Tibetan occupation by explicating a ritual manual of the fifty-eight wrathful deities from Dunhuang.

[2]What Are the Fifty-eight Wrathful Deities?

Let us begin by briefly surveying the main topic of this book, the fifty-eight wrathful deities. The one hundred peaceful and wrathful deities, or *źi khro brgya tham ba*, represent a group of divinities transmitted in the rÑiṅ ma school of Tibetan Buddhism. They are made up of forty-two peaceful deities (*źi*) and fifty-eight wrathful deities (*khro*), making a total of one hundred peaceful and wrathful deities. The rÑiṅ ma school is based on old esoteric Buddhism, transmitted during the time of the ancient Tibetan empire. Although the Tufan dynasty tried to purge the anti-social elements of late tantric Buddhism, which was flourishing in India, the esoteric teachings transmitted by Padmasambhava, Vimalamitra, and Vairocana took root among the people, and after the fall of the Tufan dynasty they became the foundation of Tibetan Buddhism.

The one hundred peaceful and wrathful deities belong to the *Māyājāla* cycle in the Kama (*bka' ma*), or Buddha's teaching, of the Mahāyoga vehicle transmitted in the rÑiṅ ma school. One of the ritual manuals of the one hundred peaceful and wrathful deities, *Źi khro dgoṅs pa raṅ grol*, was translated by Evans Wentz as the *Tibetan Book of the Dead*. In the west, the painting depicting the one hundred peaceful and wrathful deities is known as the maṇḍala of the *Tibetan Book of the Dead*. In present-day Tibet, the one hundred peaceful and wrathful deities are depicted in the form of two thangkas that are hung symmetrically, or sometimes in the form of two wall paintings, again arranged symmetrically.

In Dunhuang, on the other hand, manuscripts related to the forty-two peaceful deities and fifty-eight wrathful deities have been discovered separately. This fact suggests that at the time when the Dunhuang manuscripts were being copied, these two groups had not yet been integrated into a single system.

As I have discussed elsewhere, the forty-two peaceful deities came into existence by merging two sets of deities, namely, the deities of the *Guhyasamāja-tantra* and the *Sarvatathāgatatattvasaṃgraha*, into one system. The fifty-eight wrathful deities, on the other hand, consist of two sets of deities that are explained mainly in the *Sarvabuddhasamāyoga-tantra* (*Saṅs rgyas mñam sbyor*) and in Part II of the *Sarvatathāgatatattvasaṃgraha*. According to the rÑiṅ ma school, the *Guhyasamāja* and *Sarvabuddhasamāyoga* are included in the eighteen tantras (*sDe pa bco brgyad*) of the Mahāyoga cycle, and we may suppose that these tantras are the earliest of late tantric Buddhism and had already come into existence prior to the first propagation (*sṅa dar*) of Buddhism in Tibet.

For reference, a photograph of the maṇḍala of the fifty-eight wrathful deities in the possession of Toga Meditation Museum, Toyama prefecture, where I am chief curator, has been chosen for the front cover. A list of the deities is given on pp.68-69 and the arrangement of the deities is shown in the diagram on p. 7.

[3]Outline of the Text

Up until now, three manuscripts on the fifty-eight wrathful deities have been identified. They are IOL Tib J 332 and 716 in the possession of the British Library and Pelliot No. 321 at the Bibliothèque nationale de France.

IOL Tib J 716 is written in cursive *dbu med* script on the back of a scroll of a Chinese sūtra, and it can be divided into three parts.[1] Part I explains the visualization of the enlightened mind (*bodhicitta*) and has no relation to the fifty-eight wrathful deities. Part II, on the other hand, describes eighteen deities consisting of Heruka, the main deity, his consort Krodheśvarī, eight goddesses beginning with Gaurī, and eight animal-headed goddesses called *phra men ma* in Tibet. At the start, it says, "On the procedure how to accomplish the glorious Heruka as the deity of action" (*dpal chen po śri he ru ka las kyi lhar bskyur* [sic] *ba'i thabs la*). This may be the title of this text. Part III also explains the generation of the wrathful goddesses. However, the names of these deities differ from those of the current fifty-eight wrathful deities, and this should therefore be regarded as a separate text.

Pelliot No. 321, meanwhile, is a *pe cha* manuscript written in *dbu can* script. It consists of 24 folia and is the largest of the ritual manuals on the fifty-eight wrathful deities so far identified from Dunhuang. As for its contents, it is interesting in that it explains the significance of subjugation (*abhicāraka*). However, this manuscript ends at fol. 24b, and subsequent fragments have not been found.

IOL Tib J 332 is also a *pe cha* manuscript, consisting of 22 folia. It is complete and written in fairly clear *dbu med* script when compared with IOL Tib J 716, but it has several lacunae due to scribal errors. It is a valuable source for learning about the old tantric school during the Tibetan empire since the iconography and visualization of the fifty-eight wrathful deities it describes are almost identical to those transmitted by the present-day rÑiṅ ma school.

In addition to the above manuscripts, there also exist many Tibetan fragments of ritual manuals that mention Heruka and *ḍākinī*s. At present, it is not clear whether they belong to Part II of the *Sarvatathāgatatattvasaṃgraha*, to the *Sarvabuddhasamāyoga* or to the old tantric school of Tibet.

In the following, I shall survey the fifty-eight wrathful deities of the old tantric school, mainly on the basis of IOL Tib 332, but also with reference to IOL Tib 716 and Pelliot No. 321 as necessary.

[4]Contents of IOL Tib J 332

Next, I shall survey the contents of the manuscript. It contains several misspellings, and other discrepancies with the standard orthographical practice of classical Tibetan have been transcribed as they are. It should be noted that *kha'* indicates that *'a* (so-called small *a* or *a chung*) occurs immediately after *kha*, while *kh'a* means that a small *'a* has been written just below *kha*.

(1)Introduction

After having taken refuge in Heruka, "One should carefully explain deity yoga (*lha'i rnal 'byor*) in accordance with tantras such as the *Māyājāla* for sentient beings to generate wisdom." This comment confirms a common theory of the present-day rÑiṅ ma school that the teaching of the one hundred peaceful and wrathful deities belongs to the *Māyājāla* cycle of the Mahāyoga vehicle among the three inner vehicles.

There follows the admonition that the efforts of one who strives only to hear the teaching without pleasing the *ācārya* and without receiving initiation will be in vain. An identical verse occurs in an old tantra, the *Guhyagarbha*, which is thought to summarize the *Māyājāla* cycle of the Mahāyoga vehicle.[2] The superiority of this teaching is shown by the following statement: "This is the great secret of definitive meaning. It makes the fruit the path. Among all maṇḍalas of victors, no maṇḍala is more secret and more definitive." This is also a quotation from the *Guhyagarbha*.[3]

One should practise the meditation of the *Māyājāla* in a quiet place to calm one's mind, which is like a rutting elephant, to purify desires, to subdue the triple world, and to generate great pride (i.e., identify oneself with the deity).

(2) Meditation on equality

Next, from 1b5 to 1b6, it says, "After finishing the *sādhana* (*no pyi ka*)[4] of the maṇḍala of the wrathful deities, the meditation on equality should be performed." One should realize that all existents are by nature free from birth and cessation, and that they are inseparable from the realm (*dbyiṅs*) that is without birth and cessation.

Then, saying that "the implications of it are explained in this great tantra," a verse is quoted. This verse, too, turns out to be from the *Guhyagarbha-tantra*.[5]

In this fashion, after the visualization has been briefly explained in prose, the same process is reiterated in verse. As we shall see, these verses have in many cases been quoted from old tantras such as the *Guhyagarbha*, which were transmitted during the time of the Tibetan empire.

(3) Visualization of a sun-disc

Next, one should practise the meditation of illuminating great compassion (*kun du snaṅ sñiṅ rje chen po'i tiṅ ṅe 'dzin*).[6] A sun-disc is generated from the syllable *Ma*, and it turns empty space red. Visualization of a sun-disc as a preliminary step for the generation of wrathful deities occurs also in the *Vajrahūṅkāra-sādhanopāyikā* from Dunhuang.[7] However, in this manual Buddha-heruka, the main deity, is generated from a vajra visualized on the sun-disc. This is worth noting as a precursor of the introduction of visualization of a sun-disc in the five-stage process of enlightenment (*pañcākārābhisambodhi*) in late tantric Buddhism.

(4) Visualization of a vajra

Next, a vajra is visualized in the centre of the sun-disc from the syllable *Hūṃ*, which is reddish-brown in colour. With the mantra "*hum spha ra na Jaḥ*," rays are emitted in the ten directions and bring benefit to sentient beings. With the mantra "*saṅ ha ra na Huṅ*," the rays converge and merge into the syllable *Huṅ*. With the mantra "*va jra ti sta ti sta* (*sic*)," this syllable is transformed into a five-pronged vajra.

(5) Generation of Buddha-heruka

Next, with the mantra "*Oṃ 'bu ta śi ri he ru ka huṃ*," one becomes Buddha-heruka. It is worth noting that it is stated that, on the level of supreme truth, Buddha-heruka does not move from the peaceful (*śānta*) *dharmatākāya* (*chos ñid kyi sku*) even though he is endowed with the nine tastes (*navarasa*).[8]

(6) Realm of cilia and pavilion made of skull cups

Next, with the mantra "*ra rag ta ra rag ta*" and the seed syllable *Ra*, red like polished coral, one should visualize the realm of cilia (*lva kloṅ*) of blood, the size of which is like the universe. Its eastern cilia whirl southward, the southern cilia westward, and the western cilia northward. Next, with the mantra "*Ba Ba*," one should visualize a maṇḍala pavilion made of skull cups (*ban 'da*). This pavilion has no border between inside and outside since it covers all ten directions. In this way, the pavilion of the maṇḍala is visualized in the bloody realm of cilia, while Mt. Sumeru is visualized as the spine in the midst of the burning fire of wisdom.

(7) Visualization of a four-spoked wheel and eulogy

With the mantra "*'Bruṅ byi śva byi śud de*," one should visualize the maṇḍala, which is square, adorned with four gates and double corridors, and decorated with scull cups, snakes, sun and moon discs, and corpses, both fresh and rotten. The reference to "double corridors" means that this maṇḍala has a double pavilion consisting of an inner pavilion depicting Buddhist deities beginning with the Herukas of the five families and an outer pavilion depicting twenty-eight *dbaṅ phyug ma*s adopted from Hinduism.

On the four spokes of a wheel, one should visualize Gandharva (east),

Yakṣa (south), Rākṣasa (west), and Yama (north) couples who have been seized by the nails of the king of bulls (east), a winged buffalo greyish black in colour (south), a leopard (west), and a tiger (north), respectively. This arrangement of demigods is also based on the *Guhyagarbha*.

There have been discovered at Dunhuang maṇḍalas that depict animals in the four gates, such as EO.3579 in the possession of Musée Guimet, and manuscripts that describe four animals in the four gates of a maṇḍala. These arrangements do not tally completely with the present text, but animals arranged in the four gates of a maṇḍala may have been influenced by the old tantric school of Tibetan Buddhism.

A verse reiterates the visualization of the four-spoked wheel and the maṇḍala, and this verse, too, turns out to have been quoted from the *Guhyagarbha*.[9]

(8) Generation of Krodheśvarī

Next, one becomes the king of wrathful deities, who symbolizes the body, speech, and mind of all tathāgatas. With the mantra "*Hi Hi*," one visualizes his consort Krodheśvarī (Kro ti śva ri) on the left. Krodheśvarī's iconography is the same as that of the main deity Buddha-heruka, but she is not wearing a diadem. With the four-syllable mantra "*'Ja Huṃ Pan Ho*," one should summon, induct, bind, and delight the main deity, whereupon his *bodhicitta* (semen) falls into his consort's space (*mkh'a*), or vagina.

After having recited the verse of generation, with the mantra "*Huṃ Huṃ byi śva gro ti jva la man 'da la phat phat ha la ha la*," one visualizes all six destinies in the ten directions filled with wrathful deities holding various weapons. This passage also has a close parallel in the *Guhyagarbha*.[10]

(9) Generation of four Herukas and Bhagavat Mahāsukha

From among these deities there are born innumerable Vajra-herukas in the east, Ratna-herukas in the south, Padma-herukas in the west, and Karma-herukas in the north.

In his hands equal in number to the dust motes of a universe of one hundred million worlds Bhagavat Mahāsukha (dGyes chen po) holds weapons also equal in number to the dust motes of a universe of one hundred million worlds. His legs, also equal in number to the dust motes of a universe of one hundred million worlds, trample upon Maheśvara and his consort, with his right leg stretched out and his left leg bent (*brkyaṅ skum*).

These wrathful deities are of extremely fearful appearance, shout loudly, are three-headed, six-armed, and four-legged, and trample upon Gandharva (east), Yakṣa (south), Rākṣasa (west), and Yama (north) couples, respectively, with their right legs stretched out and their left legs bent. Here, it is stated that all the wrathful deities are three-headed, six-armed, and four-legged. This is inconsistent with the above description of Bhagavat Mahāsukha as having innumerable arms and legs. Therefore, the descriptor "three-headed, six-armed, and four-legged" presumably refers not to Bhagavat Mahāsukha but to the four Herukas generated in the four directions.

In the rÑiṅ ma school there has been transmitted a form of Heruka called Che mchog Heruka, who is considered to embody the fifty-eight wrathful deities. His iconography is similar to that of Bhagavat Mahāsukha as described here. This Che mchog Heruka presumably has his origins in a deity such as

Bhagavat Mahāsukha.

The innumerable Herukas generated in the east combine to become one, producing the figure of Vajra-heruka. In the same way, the Herukas generated in the south, west, and north combine to become one, producing the figures of Ratna-heruka, Padma-heruka, and Karma-heruka respectively and occupy their respective seats in the four directions.

(10) Generation of four Krodheśvarīs

Next, with the mantra "*gro ti śva ri 'Ja Huṃ Pam Ho*," one should visualize their consorts Krodheśvarī to the left of the main deity. Today, the fifty-eight wrathful deities, four Herukas, and four Krodheśvarīs form couples in the *yab-yum* (father and mother) style of later times, but in this text the consorts are visualized to the left (viewer's right) of the male deities. This is the same style as that of the forty-two peaceful deities discovered at Dunhuang and preserved in the Pelliot collection (EO 1144; ninth century). This would suggest that at the time when the Dunhuang manuscripts were produced the later *yab-yum* style had not yet come into existence or was at least not yet popular.

(11) Generation of Gaurī and so on

From the cloud of *bodhicitta* generated by the inseparable couple and the seed syllables "*Ha Ha Ha Ha Ha Ha Ha Ha*," seven groups of female deities starting with Gaurī (dKar mo) are generated. The verse of generation given here has a parallel in the *Guhyagarbha*.[11]

(12) Generation of animal-headed goddesses

From the cloud of *bodhicitta* generated by the inseparable couple and the seed syllables "*He He He He He He He He*," nine groups of goddesses starting with the Great Lion-headed One (Seṅ gdoṅ chen mo) are generated. The verse of generation given here also has a close parallel in the *Guhyagarbha*.[12]

(13) Generation of female gatekeepers

From the cloud of *bodhicitta* generated by the inseparable couple and the seed syllables "*Phaṭ Phaṭ Phaṭ Phaṭ*," four female gatekeepers starting with Adamantine Long Walker (rDo rje bsriṅs 'gro ma) are generated. The verse given here is not found in the *Guhyagarbha*, but an almost identical process is explained after the generation of the animal-headed goddesses in section (12).[13]

(14) Cloud of fearful goddesses

Furthermore, from the cloud of *bodhicitta* generated by the inseparable couple and the seed syllable "*Phat*," a cloud of extremely fearful goddesses is generated.

(15) Spontaneous accomplishment

Next, one should practise spontaneous accomplishment (*lhun gyis grub pa*). The process is as follows. From the *bodhicitta* of the inseparable *yab-yum* couple, the light of wisdom emanates and purifies one's body, speech, and mind. *Bodhicitta* becomes like heated gold, and with the syllables "*Oṃ Āḥ Hūṃ*" the string of three syllables (together with *bodhicitta*) melts into one's heart. From the heart, it melts the space (*mkh'a*) of the consort via the adamantine path (*rdo rje lam* = urethra) and becomes dharma-nature. From this stratum (*dbyiṅs*), the mantras and *hṛdaya*s of the maṇḍala deities are born. This process resembles the *utpattikrama* of the Jñānapāda school of the *Guhyasamāja-tantra*, which I have already described elsewhere.[14]

(16) Mantras of *śūnyatājñānavajra*, four wisdoms, triple vajras, *anurāgana*, and *pūjā*

Next, the mantras of *śūnyatājñānavajra*, *ādarśajñāna*, *pratyavekṣaṇajñāna*, *samatājñāna*, *kṛtyānuṣṭhānajñāna*, empowerment of the vajras of body, speech, and mind, *anurāgana*, and *pūjā* are given together with their translations. Among these mantras, the order of *pratyavekṣaṇajñāna* and *samatājñāna* is the reverse of the normal order. However, the name of the mantra for *pratyavekṣajñāna* is given as *mñam ba ñid kyi ye śes chen po* while that for *samatājñāna* is given as *so so kun du rtog pa'i ye śes chen po*, which means that this text has confused these two wisdoms. This series of mantras is found in the same order in the *Guhyagarbha-tantra*.[15] The *śūnyatājñānavajra* mantra is found in *Guhyasamāja* III,[16] while the mantras of the empowerment of the vajras of body, speech, and mind, *anurāgana*, and *pūjā* are found in *Guhyasamāja* VI.[17] However, it is difficult to find the mantras of the four wisdoms except in tantras of the rÑiṅ ma school.

(17) Four limbs

At 8a5 it says, "Up to this point, one generates oneself as a son of the Victor (= Buddha). After having generated the essence of the five wisdoms and pride (of becoming the five buddhas), one should generate Victors as sons of oneself." Thus, the content of the meditation changes after this point.

This calls to mind the fact that in the Jñānapāda school of the *Guhyasamāja-tantra*, after the genesis of "causal Vajradhara" from the Samantabhadra father-and-mother in the process corresponding to "consciousness" (*vijñāna*) among the twelve limbs of dependent origination, the attendant deities of the maṇḍala are born from "causal Vajradhara" in the process corresponding to rebirth (*jāti*).

Hereafter, the process of generating the maṇḍala pavilion and deities explained in sections (6) to (14) will be relived in sections (18) to (27) through generation by means of mantras.

A seed syllable is visualized on the tip of the five-pronged vajra (penis) of the male deity, while a sun-disc is generated by the seed syllable "*Ma*" in the eight-petalled lotus in the space (vagina) of the consort, Next, with the four-syllable *vidyā* "'*Dz'a Hūṃ Pam H'o*," one should summon, induct, bind, and delight the male deity's symbol, whereupon his *bodhicitta* (semen) falls into his consort's space (*mkh'a*), or vagina.

Furthermore, four places on the consort should be established by the four limbs of service (*bsñen pa'i yan lag bźi*), and a verse from the *Guhyagarbha* is quoted. Generally, the four limbs of service refer to *sevā*, *upasādhana*, *sādhana*, and *mahāsādhana* as explained in the *Guhyasamāja*. However, this text does not explain their specific contents.

(18) Generation of the maṇḍala

With the mantra "'*Bruṃ vyi śva vyi śud de*," the secret maṇḍala is generated. Like the maṇḍala generated in (6), it has a fearsome appearance, including the realm of cilia (*lva kloṅ*) of blood, the spine of Mt. Sumeru, and a pavilion made of skull cups.

(19) Generation of Buddha-heruka

With the mantra "*Oṃ 'bu da śri he ru ka ma ha tsan ta sa rva dus stan da ka ha na pa tsa Hūṃ Phat*," Buddha-heruka is visualized in the centre of the maṇḍala. He is smoky black in colour, three-faced, and six-armed and tramples on the couple Demoness (*bdud ma*) and Rudra. His first right hand holds a universe of one hundred million worlds with a somma (*cakravāḍa*), his second right hand a vajra, his third right hand a plough of wisdom, his first left hand an axe, his second left hand a sword, and his third left hand a plough of wisdom. He is accompanied on his left by his consort Krodheśvarī in the likeness of her spouse.

(20) Generation of Vajra-heruka

Then, with the mantra "*Oṃ va jra ma ha śri he ru k'a sa rva dus stan da ka ha na pa tsa Hūṃ Phat/ Oṃ dar ma kro ti śva ri Hūṅ Phat,*" Vajra-heruka is visualized on the spoke in the east of the maṇḍala. He is blue-black in colour, three-faced, and six-armed and holds a Gandharva couple with the fangs of a *garuḍa*. Like Buddha-heruka, his first right hand holds a universe of one hundred million worlds with a somma, his second right hand a vajra, his third right hand a plough of wisdom, his first left hand an axe, his second left hand a sword, and his third left hand a plough of wisdom. He is accompanied on his left by his consort (Vajra-)krodheśvarī in the likeness of her spouse.

(21) Generation of Ratna-heruka

Then, with the mantra "*Oṃ rad na ma ha śri he ru ka ma ha can dha sa rva du śtan da ka ha na pa tsa Hūṃ Phat/ Oṃ su rya rad na kro ti śva ri Hūṃ Phat,*" Ratna-heruka is visualized on the spoke in the south of the maṇḍala. He is yellowish black in colour, three-faced, and six-armed and holds a Yakṣa couple with the fangs of a winged buffalo. His first right hand holds a universe of one hundred million worlds with a somma, his second right hand a vajra, his third right hand a skull cup filled with blood, his first left hand an axe, his second left hand a sword, and his third left hand a plough of wisdom. He is accompanied on his left by his consort Ratna-krodheśvarī in the likeness of her spouse.

(22) Generation of Padma-heruka

Then, with the mantra "*Oṃ pad ma śri he ru ga ma ha tsan da sa rva du stan da ka ha na pa tsa Hūṃ Phat/ Oṃ hri śa ta pa ka ma/ ma ha kro ti śva ri byi śa byi śud de Hūṃ Phat*," Padma-heruka is visualized on the spoke in the west of the maṇḍala. He is reddish black in colour, three-faced, and six-armed and holds a Rākṣasa couple with the fangs of a leopard. His first right hand holds a universe of one hundred million worlds with a somma, his second right hand a vajra, his third right hand a skull cup filled with blood, his first left hand an axe, his second left hand a sword, and his third left hand a plough of wisdom. He is accompanied on his left by his consort Padma-krodheśvarī in the likeness of her spouse.

(23) Generation of Karma-heruka

Then, with the mantra "*Oṃ kar ma ma ha śri he ru ka ma ha tsan da sa rva du śtan da ka ha na pa tsa Hūṃ Phat/ Oṃ ma ha a mo ka Hūṃ Phat*," Karma-heruka is visualized on the spoke in the north of the maṇḍala. He is greenish black in colour, three-faced, and six-armed and holds a Yama couple with the fangs of a tiger. His first right hand holds a universe of one hundred million worlds with a somma, his second right hand a vajra, his third right hand a skull cup filled with blood, his first left hand an axe, his second left hand a sword, and his third left hand a plough of wisdom. He is accompanied on his

Table 1. Iconography of Eight Female Deities Beginning with Gaurī

Name	Direc-tion	IOL Tib J 332			IOL Tib J 716			Pelliot No.321		
		Colour	Right Hand	Left Hand	Colour	Right Hand	Left Hand	Colour	Right Hand	Left Hand
Gaurī	E	blue	swinging staff of corpse	kapāla	blue	staff of corpse	kapāla	blue	staff of corpse	conch shell filled with blood
Caurī	S	yellow	fitting arrow to string of bow		yellow	fitting arrow to string of bow		yellow	fitting arrow to string of bow	
Pramohā	W	red	holding makara-topped banner		red	holding makara-topped banner		red	holding makara-topped banner	
Vetālī	N	black	brandishing vajra with right hand, holding waist of corpse with left hand and devouring it		black	vajra	holding corpse and devouring it	black	vajra	holding corpse and devouring it
Pukkasī	SE	reddish yellow	holding head of corpse with right hand, plucking bowels and fat with left hand and devouring them		description missing			reddish yellow	plucking vasuta from corpse and devouring it	
Ghasmarī	SW	green	holding kapāla filled with blood with her left hand and drinking it with nine-pronged vajra in right hand		illegible			green	stirring blood and drinking it from kapāla	kapāla
Śmaśānī	NW	dark blue	holding legs of corpse with right hand, head with left hand, and plucking heart from corpse with teeth		description missing			blue	holding head and tail of corpse with both hands	
Caṇḍālī	NE	pale yellow	holding waist of corpse with left hand, cutting whole skeleton with right hand and offering it to main deity		description missing			reddish black	kapāla	holding corpse

left by his consort Karma-krodheśvarī in the likeness of her spouse.

(24) Generation of eight female deities beginning with Gaurī

Then, with the mantra "va jra ge'u ri ha," Gaurī is visualized on a corpse in the east outside the maṇḍala. She is blue in colour, one-headed, and two-armed. She is holding up a staked dead body with her right hand and is drinking blood from a skull cup held in her left hand. Caurī, Pramohā, and Vetālī are visualized in the south, west, and north, respectively, and in the four corners Pukkasī, Ghasmarī, Śmaśānī, and Caṇḍālī are visualized in the southeast, southwest, northwest, and northeast, respectively. These eight goddesses appear in the Samāyoga-tantra, one of the earliest Mother tantras. Among these goddesses, the Sanskrit equivalent of Sme śa can had been unclear since some texts have Śmaśānī and other texts have Ḍombī. In this text, the mantra of this goddess is given as "va jra sma śa ni," as in the Guhyagarbha-tantra, and this suggests that Śmaśānī is correct.

IOL Tib J 716 and Pelliot No. 321 also mention eight goddesses beginning with Gaurī. However, due to an error on the part of the scribe, the descriptions of the goddesses from Ghasmarī to Heron-headed (Kaṅ ka) among the eight animal-headed goddesses is missing in IOL Tib J 716. The descriptions in these three manuscripts are compared in Table 1. The descriptions of the iconography of Gaurī and so on in the three manuscripts are very similar, and their present-day iconography in the rÑiṅ ma school is also not so different. Therefore, the iconography of the eight goddesses beginning with Gaurī seems to have already become fixed during the time of the Tibetan empire.

(25)Generation of eight animal-headed goddesses beginning with Seṅ gdoṅ

Further outside the maṇḍala, eight animal-headed goddesses beginning with Lion-headed (Seṅ gdoṅ) are visualized. However, because of a lacuna here, details of the iconography of Seṅ gdoṅ are not given. Next, Tiger-headed (sTag gdoṅ) is red in colour, one-headed, and two-armed. Forming a mudrā with both hands crossed at her shoulders, she is devouring the heart of a corpse with her teeth. In the west and north, Fox-headed (Sri la) and Dog-headed (Śva na) are visualized, and in the four corners Eagle-headed (Kri ta), Heron-headed (Kaṅ ka), Crow-headed (Ka ka), and Owl-headed (U lu) goddesses are visualized in the southeast, southwest, northwest, and northeast, respectively. The names of these goddesses coincide with those in the present-day fifty-eight wrathful deities of the rÑiṅ ma school.

In IOL Tib J 716, on the other hand, only three goddesses starting with Heron-headed (Kaṅ ka) are described. The descriptions in the three manuscripts

Table 2. Iconography of Eight Animal-headed Goddesses

Name	IOL Tib J 332				IOL Tib J 716			Pelliot No.321		
	Direc-tion	Colour	Right Hand	Left Hand	Colour	Right Hand	Left Hand	Colour	Right Hand	Left Hand
Lion headed	E	description missing			description missing			yellow	forming vajra-fist with both hands on her shoulder and biting a corpse	
Tiger headed	S	red	forming *mudrā* with both hands on her shoulder and plucking heart from corpse with her teeth		description missing			red	crossing her both hands over decomposed corpse *'bri tshugs su lta ba* (nonsensical)	
Fox headed	W	black	skinning corpse with both hands and making it into matting		description missing			black	breaking corpse with both hands and chewing it	
Dog headed	N	blue black	trampling on head of corpse with right leg, on legs with left leg and devouring fat and intestines		description missing			black	holding corpse with both hand and breaking it	
Eagle headed	SE	red	*kapāla*	holding razor	description missing			reddish black	holding sword	*kapāla*
Heron headed	SW	yellow	skinning corpse with both hands and slinging its legs on her shoulder		reddish white	carrying corpse on left shoulder		reddish white	sword	carrying corpse on shoulder
Crow headed	NW	black	*kapāla*	holding razor	black	*padma-bhājana*	curved knife	black	sword	*kapāla*
Owl headed	NE	maroon	*kapāla*	summoning with vajra-hook	multi-colour-ed	conch shell filled with blood	vajra-hook	green	holding hook	*kapāla*

are compared in Table 2. Considerable differences can be seen between the Dunhuang manuscripts and the present-day iconography of the rÑiṅ ma school regarding the iconography of the eight animal-headed goddesses. In the case of the four goddesses starting with Eagle-headed, the attributes of the right and left hands in Pelliot No. 321 are the reverse of those in IOL Tib J 332 and 716. This may be due to confusion of the goddesses' right and left hands and right and left when facing the canvas, and it suggests that the composer of the ritual manual referred to some icons or drawings that existed in Dunhuang.

(26)Generation of four female gatekeepers

In the outside eastern gate, Horse-headed Aṅkuśī (rTa gdoṅ lcags kyu ma) is generated. She is white in colour and holds a hook in her right hand and a razor in her left hand. Boar-headed Pāśī, Sun-and-Moon-Eyed (Ñi zla spyan), and Ash Ghaṇṭā (Thal byed dril bus ma) are visualized in the southern, western, and

A Ritual Manual of the Fifty-eight Wrathful Deities

Table 3. Iconography of Four Gatekeptresses

Name	IOL Tib J 332				Pelliot No.321			
	Gate	Colour	Right Hand	Left Hand	Gate	Colour	Right Hand	Left Hand
Horse headed Aṅkuśī	E	white	hook	razor	E	blue	hook	*kapāla*
Boar headed Pāśī	S	blue	noose	showing boar's tusk	S	blue-black	boar's tusk	*kapāla*
Sun and moon eye	W	red	*vajra*	hook (writing error for chain?)	W	dark red	vajra-chain	*kapāla*
Ash Ghaṇṭā	N	green	vajra-bell	vajra-hook	N	?	ringing vajra-bell	*kapāla*

northern gates, respectively. Their names also appear in the *Samāyoga-tantra*. The Sanskrit equivalent of Thal byed in the northern gate had been unclear, but in this text the mantra of this goddess is given as *"va jra pa smyi ba la te ho,"* as in the *Guhyagarbha-tantra*. Pelliot No. 321, on the other hand, has *"va jra pa smyi pa la ya ho,"* and this suggests that Vajrabhasmī is correct.[18]

IOL Tib J 716 does not describe the four female gatekeepers. Accordingly, only the descriptions given in this manuscript and Pelliot No. 321 have been compared in Table 3.

(27) Genaration of twenty-eight *dbaṅ phyug ma*s

Still further outside, the twenty-eight *dbaṅ phyug ma*s are visualized with the seed syllable *"Bhyo."* There are six in each of the four directions and one in each of the four gates. This arrangement coincides with the present-day fifty-eight wrathful deities of the rÑiṅ ma school. Today, all twenty-eight *dbaṅ phyug ma*s have animal heads. However, IOL Tib J 332 does not stipulate animal heads except for Grub mo, the third in the west, who has a fox's head;

52

Chu'i lha mo, the sixth in the north, who has the head of a *makara* (sea monster); and Ra mgo ma in the southern gate, who has a goat's head. 'Tsaṅs ma (Brahmā's consort), the second in the east, is described as having four (human) heads like Brahmā in Hinduism. Therefore, the other *dbaṅ phyug ma*s presumably have human heads.

As I have discussed elsewhere, the twenty-eight *dbang phyug ma*s consist of the consorts of twenty deities mentioned in Part II of the *Sarvatathāgata-tattvasaṃgraha* and eight additional goddesses (including Umā, the consort of Maheśvara).[19] However, the consorts of the twenty deities mentioned in the *Sarvatathāgatatattvasaṃgraha* are basically rendered as human-headed goddesses.[20] These facts suggest that the twenty-eight *dbaṅ phyug ma*s with animal heads had not yet come into existence at the time of the Dunhuang manuscripts. Even though Pelliot No. 321 is a quite voluminous work, it does not explain the iconography of the twenty-eight *dbaṅ phyug ma*s, at least not in its extant parts.

The names and arrangement of the twenty-eight *dbaṅ phyug ma*s in this text, the *Guhyagarbha*, and the consorts of the twenty deities mentioned in Part II of the *Sarvatathāgatatattvasaṃgraha* are given in table on p.69. This table shows that the names and arrangement of the twenty-eight *dbaṅ phyug ma*s are closer to the *Guhyagarbha-tantra* than to present-day ritual manuals of the *gter ma* cycle. However, as regards their body colours and attributes, which the *Guhyagarbha* does not describe in detail, some of the descriptions in the present text coincide with present-day ritual manuals.

These facts suggest that this text dates from a transitional stage in the process of development from the early stage of the cult of mother goddesses in late tantric Buddhism to the present-day fifty-eight wrathful deities.

A Ritual Manual of the Fifty-eight Wrathful Deities

(28) Summoning the maṇḍala

Next, it says, "What does it symbolize? It should be interpreted in accordance with this tantra." Then, quoting from the *Guhyagarbha*,[21] the special characteristics of this maṇḍala are explained. Next, the mantra for summoning the deities of the maṇḍala, "*Oṃ ru lu ru lu ru lu huṅ bhyo va jra sa ma ya ho// va jra sa ma ya stvam/ va jra sa ma ya ho*," is given.

It then says, "Now, this song for accomplishment is performed," and a eulogy of the wrathful deities and the mantra "*Oṃ sa ma ya Oṃ//va jra sa ma ya phaṭ/Ram ā li u li ta li ta pa to śa/ śam mgo na ru ti kha ram yo gi ni Huṅ Hā He Phaṭ*" are given. This song for accomplishment is also quoted from the *Guhyagarbha-tantra*.[22]

(29) Emergence of the maṇḍala

The maṇḍala is clearly arranged, and there appears a blazing maṇḍala which covers all of the six destinies in the ten directions. There follows a verse describing the iconography of the main deity, Heruka. This verse turns out to be a quotation from the *Guhyagarbha*.[23]

Next, quoting the *Guhyagarbha* again, it says, "the maṇḍala equipped with all limbs and equipment and (performed by the yogin) who thoroughly knows the ritual manuals and has accumulated yogic practice fulfils attainments in all actions."[24] It continues, "Now, this song for accomplishment is performed," and one should recite the eulogy of the wrathful deities. This song is also quoted from the *Guhyagarbha*.[25]

(30) Reduction (*anubheda*) of the maṇḍala

Next, the reduction of the maṇḍala is explained, saying that one should now reduce the maṇḍala of great flames and one's own *skandha-dhātv-āyatana*. The process is as follows: 1) one's own *skandha-dhātv-āyatana* is reduced to the syllable *Hūṃ*; 2) this *Hūṃ* is reduced to *Hā*, the nature of which is Vairocana or *viśuddhadharmadhātujñāna*, to *ṅa* or the *anusvāra* (diacritic dot used to mark a type of nasal sound), the nature of which is Ratnasambhava or *samatājñāna*, to *'a* or the macron, the nature of which is Amitābha or *pratyavekṣaṇajñāna*, to *źabs skyed* (= *źabs kyu*: vowel *u* below a syllable), the nature of which is Amoghasiddhi or *kṛtyānuṣṭhānajñāna*, and to *thig le* or *nāda*, the nature of which is Vajrasattva or *ādarśajñāna*. If they are assigned to the triple mysteries, *Ha* is the nature of the body, *źabs skyed* the nature of speech, and *thig le* the nature of mind.

Then *źabs skyed* melts into the macron, the macron melts into *Ha*, *Ha* melts into the *anusvāra*, *Ha* and *ṅa* melt into *zla tshes* (*candrabindu*), and *ṅa* melts into *thig le* (*nāda*). And with the understanding that *thig le* and *dharmakāya* are inseparable, one remains in this state of deliverance for as long as one wishes.

This visualization is very similar to the *anubheda* peculiar to the late Saṃvara cycle.[26] But in the late Saṃvara cycle the syllable *Hūṃ* breaks down into six components: 1) vowel mark, 2) character representing consonants, 3) head of a syllable (*sirorekhā*), 4) crescent-shaped ornament (*candrabindu*), 5) nasal dot (*anusvāra*), and 6) *nāda*. In this text, on the other hand, the macron peculiar to the Tibetan script has been added and *sirorekhā* is omitted. *Anubheda* was thought to be more recent since it is characteristic of the late Saṃvara cycle, but it turns out to date from the ninth century at the latest.

This section ends with "*Namo*, the method of practice named adornment of the supreme appearance of truth (*na mo de kho na ñid kyi snaṅ ba dam pa*

A Ritual Manual of the Fifty-eight Wrathful Deities

rgyan gi bsgom thabs) is finished." This suggests that an independent visualization of *anubheda* was incorporated into the ritual manual of the fifty-eight wrathful deities.

(31) Invitation of deities

Clearly visualizing the maṇḍala, one should draw the maṇḍala of great fear towards oneself. Quoting the *Great Tantra*, one should invite all the deities into the maṇḍala.

(32) Settlement in the maṇḍala

Next, praising Heruka, Krodheśvarī, and inner and outer Ḍākinīs with verses, one should request them to settle firmly in the maṇḍala.

(33) Offering of five ambrosias

Then, praising the Herukas of the five families, the Krodheśvarīs of the five families, the eight female deities beginning with Gaurī, the eight animal-headed goddesses, the four female gatekeepers, and the inner and outer Vajrārali, one should offer them the five ambrosias (*sman pan tsa a 'bri ta*).

(34) Symbols of the deities

Before the offering of the five ambrosias, there appear a dance of flames and mudrās. Then, the iconography of the eight female deities beginning with Gaurī, the eight animal-headed goddesses, and the four female gate keepers is described in verse. The verses explaining the body colours and symbols of the eight female deities beginning with Gaurī turn out to have parallels in the tantra *Khrag thuṅ 'dus pa* included in the *rÑiṅ ma rgyud 'bum*.[27]

(35) Confession

Confession and repentance should now be performed in front of the maṇḍala of great fear. One must repent in verse of faults committed during the procedure and pray for pardon.

(36) Visualization of wheels of the four elements

With the syllables "*Ram Ram*" one should visualize the wheel of fire, with which all karmic imprints of passions are burnt up. Next, with the syllables "*Yam Yam*" one should visualize the wheel of wind on the wheel of earth in the shape of a crossed vajra (*rgya gram dbaṅ chen* = *mahīndra*), and all the burnt ash is blown away. Then, with the syllables "*Khaṅ Khaṅ*" one should visualize the wheel of water and thoroughly wash away the remaining dirt with it.

This type of visualization of wheels of the four elements is also found in manuscripts of Chinese esoteric Buddhism from Dunhuang.[28]

(37) Allocation of seed-syllables of the five buddhas

Next, for decorating the five paths (*lam rgyud lṅa*), one should visualize the syllable "*Oṃ*" on the crown of the head, "*Hūṃ*" on the ears, "*Am*" in the nose, "*Svā*" on the navel, and "*Ha*" on the tongue. These syllables are frequently used as the seed-syllables of the five buddhas Vairocana, Akṣobhya, Ratnasambhava, Amitābha, and Amoghasiddhi in the *Guhyasamāja* cycle. However, in the *Guhyasamāja* cycle, Vairocana is usually assigned to the crown of the head or between the eyebrows, Akṣobhya to the heart, Amitābha to the mouth or throat, Ratnasambhava to the navel, and Amoghasiddhi to both legs.[29]

According to the verse given in this text, if one allocates the seed-syllables of the five buddhas, there is nothing to be afraid of since one becomes immortal,

A Ritual Manual of the Fifty-eight Wrathful Deities

for it is an offering of the five aggregates, the abode of consciousness, to the five buddhas.

(38) Admonishment and conclusion

Then the *ācārya* should recite some verses that are also quoted from the *Guhyagarbha.*[30] It is worth noting that they end as follows: "Reality, originally unborn, is like an illusion, an appearance, and a mirage, and even if one practises all kinds of sexual intercourse (*sbyor*) and subjugation (*sgrol*), one has not done anything." Sexual intercourse and subjugation were regarded as evil deeds typical of the old tantric school, but this verse provides justification for them.

At 22b3 it says, "*rdzogs sts-ho,*" indicating that the text ends here. But there follow several lines of mantras for *abhiṣeka* and so on.

[5]Conclusion

As shown above, the esoteric Buddhist manuscripts IOL Tib J 332, 716 and Pelliot Tibetan No. 321 from Dunhuang are ritual manuals of the fifty-eight wrathful deities of the old tantric school of Tibet transmitted during the time of the Tibetan empire. In particular, IOL Tib J 332 is the most important since it tallies with the ritual manuals and icons of the fifty-eight wrathful deities transmitted by the present-day rÑiṅ ma school. It is also valuable for the many quotations from old tantras such as the *Guhyagarbha* that have been identified. It is an indispensable text since there are few reliable materials about the old tantric school during the Tufan dynasty.

As I have discussed elsewhere, the fifty-eight wrathful deities are a synthesis of deities expounded in the *Sarvabuddhasamāyoga*, one of the earliest Mother tantras, and the mothers or consorts of twenty Hindu deities explained in Part II of the *Sarvatathāgatatattvasaṃgraha*.[31] This text preserves some early aspects, and we can surmise that it belongs to a transitional stage in developments from the early stages of the mother goddess cult in tantric Buddhism to the present-day fifty-eight wrathful deities.

With regard to the generation of deities, it describes the so-called sexo-yogic generation of deities peculiar to late tantric Buddhism, and parts of this process are similar to that of the Jñānapāda school of the *Guhyasamāja-tantra* which I have discussed elsewhere. This would seem to support the view that an early form of the Jñānapāda school had already been introduced during the Tufan dynasty. It is also worth noting that a primitive form of *anubheda* visualization peculiar to the late Saṃvara cycle is also found in this text.

Therefore, this text is important not only for learning about the origins of the rÑiṅ ma school of Tibetan Buddhism, but also for considering the historical development of late Indian tantric Buddhism. It is for this reason that the manuscript has been reproduced in Tibetan in the following pages. There exist several misspellings in the manuscript, and these and other discrepancies with standard orthographical practice of classical Tibetan have been reproduced as they are.

I would like to continue my study of the transmission and development of tantric Buddhism in Dunhuang through the analysis of Tibetan esoteric Buddhist manuscripts. And I also hope to clarify the relationship between the old tantric school transmitted during the time of the ancient empire of Tibet and the present-day rÑiṅ ma school of Tibetan Buddhism.

A Ritual Manual of the Fifty-eight Wrathful Deities

Notes

1) See The Seminar on Tibet, *A Catalogue of the Tibetan Manuscripts Collected by Sir Aurel Stein*, vol. 8 (Tokyo: The Toyo Bunko, 1984), 35-37. We had already input almost all the data in preparation for publishing a revised edition, but for various reasons it was not able to be published.

2) Peking No. 455, Vol. 10, 5-3-2～3. An alternative version (No. 457) is included in the Peking edition, and most of the quotations are found in both versions. In the following, only correspondences with No. 455 are given.

3) Peking No. 455, Vol. 10, 6-3-2～4.

4) "*no pyi ka*" is probably the second half of *sādhanopāyikā*, with *nopāyikā* having been wrongly interpreted as *sādhana*.

5) Peking No. 455, Vol. 10, 1-4-5～6.

6) Among Dunhuang manuscripts, IOL Tib J 436 I and 554 also explain *kun tu snaṅ gi tiṅ ṅe 'dzin* as one of the three *samādhi*s of Mahāyoga, but it is not clear whether they are identical with this text.

7) Kimiaki Tanaka, *Essays on Tantric Buddhism in Dunhuang: Its Art and Texts* (Kyoto: Hōzōkan, 2000), 135-149, 230-246.

8) On *navarasa* theory in Indo-Tibetan Buddhism, see Tanaka Kimiaki, "Issaibutsu shūe dakini kaimō yuga shosetsu 'kumi' kō" [A consideration of the nine sentiments (*navarasa*) found in the *Sarvabuddhasamāyogaḍākinījāla-saṃvara-tantra*], *Tōhō* (*The East*) 5 (1989): 74-84; id., "Navarasa Theory in the *Sarvabuddhasamāyogaḍākinījālasaṃvara-tantra* Reconsidered," *Tōhō* (*The East*) 10 (1994): 323-331.

9) Peking No. 455, Vol. 10, 8-2-4～6.

10) A similar process occurs at ibid. 6-5-7ff.

11) Ibid. 7-3-7~8.

12) Ibid. 7-4-1~3.

13) Ibid. 7-4-3~5.

14) Kimiaki Tanaka, *Samantabhadra nāma sādhana-ṭīkā: Introduction, Romanized Sanskrit Text and Translation* (Tokyo: Watanabe Publishing, 2017); id., *Sei to shi no mikkyō* [The sexology and thanatology of Buddhism] (Tokyo: Shunjūsha, 1997), 102-109.

15) Peking No. 455, Vol. 10, 3-4-8~5-2.

16) Matsunaga Yūkei, *Himitsu shūe tantora kōtei bonpon* [The Guhyasamāja Tantra] (Osaka: Tōhō Shuppan, 1978), 11.

17) Ibid., 17.

18) After the publication of the Sanskrit edition of the *Caryāmelāpakapradīpa*, which frequently cites the *Sarvabuddhasamāyoga*, the original Sanskrit of Thal byed ma turned out to be Bhasmapralayavetālī.

19) Tanaka Kimiaki, *Shōkai Kawaguchi Ekai korekushon-Chibetto Nepāru bukkyō bijutsu* [A catalogue of Ekai Kawaguchi's collection of Tibetan and Nepalese Buddhist art] (Tokyo: Kōsei Shuppansha, 1990), 58.

20) Icons of the consorts of the twenty Hindu deities of the Vajradhātu-maṇḍala had not been known except for a wall painting of the Trailokyavijaya-maṇḍala in the Vairocana chapel of Alchi temple in Ladakh. But a photograph of the Trilokacakra-maṇḍala in the Great Stupa of dPal 'khor chos sde monastery taken by Masaki Akira appeared in Tachikawa Musashi and Masaki Akira, *Chibetto Bukkyō zuzō kenkyū-Penkoru chūde buttō* [Iconographic studies of the stupa of Gyantse], Bulletin of the National Museum of Ethnology, special issue no. 18 (Osaka: National Museum of Ethnology, 1997), and in this example most

of the twenty consorts are depicted as ordinary or human-headed goddesses.

21) Peking No. 455, Vol. 10, 4-5-8～5-1-1.

22) Ibid. 8-2-1.

23) Ibid. 8-2-6～8.

24) Ibid. 5-4-5.

25) Ibid. 9-2-8～3-4.

26) On *anubheda*, see Okuyama Naoji, "Indo kōki mikkyō ni okeru jiko shinkaron" [Self-deification in late Indian tantric Buddhism], *Indogaku Mikkyōgaku Kenkyū* [Studies in Indology and esoteric Buddhism] (Kyoto: Hōzōkan, 1993), 809-826; Tanaka, *Sei to shi no mikkyō*, 140-141.

27) *dPal khrag 'thuṅ 'dus pa rtsa ba'i rgyud* (Kaneko No. 381), fol. 113, 1-3.

28) Kaji Tetsujō "Tonkōbon mikkyō bunken ni tsuite" [On the literature of esoteric Buddhism found in Tun-huang), in *Studies of Esoteric Buddhism and Tantrism: In Commemoration of the 1,150th Anniversary of the Founding of Koyasan* (Koyasan: Koyasan University, 1965), 223-236.

29) Kimiaki Tanaka, *The Mañjuvajramukhyākhyāna: Introduction, Romanized Sanskrit Text and Related Articles* (Tokyo: Watanabe Publishing, 2018), 20 [Japanese], 44 [English]. According to Kaji, op. cit., the visualization of these five syllables also appears in a Chinese esoteric Buddhist manuscript from Dunhuang called *Dasheng siwuliang anxin rudaofa yaolüe* 大乘四無量安心入道法要略. However, the allocation of the five syllables matches neither that of this text nor that in the *Guhyasamāja* cycle.

30) Peking No. 455, Vol. 10, 5-4-2～4.

31) Tanaka Kimiaki, *Mandara ikonorojī* [Maṇḍala iconology] (Tokyo: Hirakawa Shuppansha, 1987), 243-252. Reference should be made to the second

impression or later, in which an inappropriate explanation in the first printing has been amended.

IOL Tib J 332の科文

(1)序	1a1～1b5.
(2)平等性の三摩地	1b5～2a3.
(3)日輪観	2a3～2a5.
(4)金剛杵の観想	2a5～2b1.
(5)ブッダ・ヘールカの出生	2b1～2b4.
(6)氈毛の界とカパーラの楼閣	2b4～3a2.
(7)四輻輪の観想と讃	3a2～3b3.
(8)忿怒自在母の出生	3b3～4a4.
(9)四部ヘールカと婆伽梵大楽の出生	4a4～5a3.
(10)四忿怒自在母の出生	5a3～5a5.
(11)ガウリー等の女性尊の出生	5a5～5b3.
(12)鳥獣の頭をもつ女性尊の出生	5b3～6a3.
(13)門衛の出生	6a3～6b1.
(14)忿怒尊群の出生	6b1～6b3.
(15)任運成就観	6b3～7b1.
(16)空智金剛・四智・三金剛・随愛・供養の真言	7b1～8a3.
(17)四支	8a4～8b5.
(18)曼荼羅の生起	8b5～9a2.
(19)ブッダ・ヘールカの生起	9a2～9b1.

(20)ヴァジュラ・ヘールカの生起	9b1〜10a1.
(21)ラトナ・ヘールカの生起	10a1〜10a6.
(22)パドマ・ヘールカの生起	10a6〜10b5.
(23)カルマ・ヘールカの生起	10b5〜11a3.
(24)ガウリー等の八女尊の生起	11a3〜12a5.
(25)獅子面女等の鳥獣の頭をもつ八女尊の生起	12a5〜13b1.
(26)門衛の四女尊の生起	13b1〜14a5.
(27)二十八ワンチュクマの生起	14a5〜16b1.
(28)曼荼羅の鉤召	16b1〜16b6.
(29)曼荼羅の出現	16b6〜17b7.
(30)曼荼羅の収束(随滅)	17b7〜18b5.
(31)諸尊の招入	18b5〜19a7.
(32)曼荼羅への入住	19a7〜19b2.
(33)五甘露の奉献	19b2〜20a7.
(34)諸尊の三昧耶形	20a7〜21a3.
(35)懺悔	21a3〜21a6.
(36)四大輪の観想	21a6〜21b6.
(37)五仏の種字の布置	21b6〜22a6.
(38)教誡と結尾	22a7〜22b3.
(39)真言	22b4〜22b8.

A Ritual Manual of the Fifty-eight Wrathful Deities

Synopsis of IOL Tib J 332

(1)Introduction	1a1~1b5.
(2)Meditation on equality	1b5~2a3.
(3)Visualization of a sun-disc	2a3~2a5.
(4)Visualization of a vajra	2a5~2b1.
(5)Generation of Buddha-heruka	2b1~2b4.
(6)Realm of cilia and pavilion made of skull cups	2b4~3a2.
(7)Visualization of a four-spoked wheel and eulogy	3a2~3b3.
(8)Generation of Krodheśvarī	3b3~4a4.
(9)Generation of four Herukas and Bhagavat Mahāsukha	4a4~5a3.
(10)Generation of four Krodheśvarīs	5a3~5a5.
(11)Generation of Gaurī and so on	5a5~5b3.
(12)Generation of animal-headed goddesses	5b3~6a3.
(13)Generation of female gatekeepers	6a3~6b1.
(14)Cloud of fearful goddesses	6b1~6b3.
(15)Spontaneous accomplishment	6b3~7b1.
(16)Mantras of *Śūnyatājñānavajra*, four wisdoms, triple vajras, *anurāgana*, and *pūjā*	7b1~8a3.
(17)Four limbs	8a4~8b5.
(18)Generation of the maṇḍala	8b5~9a2.
(19)Generation of Buddha-heruka	9a2~9b1.

(20)Generation of Vajra-heruka	9b1～10a1.
(21)Generation of Ratna-heruka	10a1～10a6.
(22)Generation of Padma-heruka	10a6～10b5.
(23)Generation of Karma-heruka	10b5～11a3.
(24)Generation of eight female deities beginning with Gaurī	11a3～12a5.
(25)Generation of eight animal-headed goddesses beginning with Seṅ gdoṅ	12a5～13b1.
(26)Generation of four female gatekeepers	13b1～14a5.
(27)Generation of twenty-eight *dbaṅ phyug ma*s	14a5～16b1.
(28)Summoning the maṇḍala	16b1～16b6.
(29)Emergence of the maṇḍala	16b6～17b7.
(30)Reduction (*anubheda*) of the maṇḍala	17b7～18b5.
(31)Invitation of deities	18b5～19a7.
(32)Settlement in the maṇḍala	19a7～19b2.
(33)Offering of five ambrosias	19b2～20a7.
(34)Symbols of the deities	20a7～21a3.
(35)Confession	21a3～21a6.
(36)Visualization of wheels of the four elements	21a6～21b6.
(37)Allocation of seed-syllables of the five buddhas	21b6～22a6.
(38)Admonishment and conclusion	22a7～22b3.
(39)Mantras for *abhiṣeka* and so on	22b4～22b8.

忿怒五十八尊 (Fifty-eight Wrathful Deities) 尊名一覧表

Japanese	Sanskrit/English	IOL Tib J 332
a.チェチョクヘールカ	Mahāśrīheruka	
b.インチュク・クローデ ーシュヴ ァリー	Dhātvīśvarī	
1.ブッダ・ヘールカ	Buddha-heruka	'bu ta he ru ka
2.ヴァジュラ・ヘールカ	Vajra-heruka	va dzra śri he ru ka
3.ラトナ・ヘールカ	Ratna-heruka	rad na he ru ga
4.パドマ・ヘールカ	Padma-heruka	pad ma śri he ru ka
5.カルマ・ヘールカ	Karma-heruka	kar ma he ru ka
6.ブ ッダ ・クローデ ーシュヴ ァリー	Buddha-krodeśvarī	kro ti śva ri
7.ヴ ァジ ュラ・クローデ ーシュヴ ァリー	Vajra-krodeśvarī	kro di śva ri
8.ラトナ・クローデ ーシュヴ ァリー	Ratna-krodeśvarī	rad na kro ti śva ri
9.パ ド マ・クローデ ーシュヴ ァリー	Padma-krodeśvarī	pad ma kro ti śva ri
10.カルマ・クローデ ーシュヴ ァリー	Karma-krodeśvarī	kar ma kro ti śva ri
11.ガウリー	Gaurī	va dzra ke'u ri
12.チャウリー	Caurī	va dzra ce'u ri
13.プラモーハー	Pramohā	va dzra pra mo ha
14.ヴェーターリー	Vetalī	va dzra pe ta li
15.プッカシー	Pukkasī	va dzra pu ka si
16.ガスマリー	Ghasmarī	va dzra ka sma ri
17.チャンダーリー	Caṇḍālī	va dzra tsan da li
18.シュマシャーニー	Śmaśānī	va dzra sma śa ni
19.獅子面女	Lion headed	[siṃ ha]
20.虎面女	Tiger headed	va dzra vya kri mu kha
21.狐面女	Fox headed	va dzra sri la
22.狗面女	Dog headed	va dzra śva na mu kha
23.鷲頭女	Eagle headed	va dzra kri ta mu kha
24.鷺頭女	Heron headed	va dzra kaṅ ka mu kha
25.烏頭女	Crow headed	va dzra kha kha mu kha
26.梟頭女	Owl headed	va dzra hu lu mu kha
27.馬頭鉤女	Horse headed Aṅkuśī	rta gdoṅ lcags kyu ma
28.猪頭索女	Boar headed Pāśī	phag gdoṅ źags pa ma
29.日月目女	Sun and moon eye	rdo rje ñi zla spyan
30.灰鈴女	Ash Ghaṇṭa	thal byed dril bus ma

28ワンチュクマ(28 dbaṅ phyug mas)尊名一覧表

gSaṅ ba'i sñiṅ po	Twenty mothers (STTS)	IOL Tib J 332
31.dmar mo		1.myi'i srin mo
32.tshaṅs ma	3.Brahmāṇī	2.'tsaṅs ma
33.'khrug mo	Umā	3.khro mo
34.'jug sred mo	1.Rukmiṇī	5.'jug sred
35.gźon nu ma	2.Ṣaṣṭhī	6.gźo(*sic*) nu
36.dbaṅ mo	4.Indrāṇī	4.dbaṅ mo
37.rdo rje ser mo	8.Jātahāriṇī	9.rdo rje dmar mo
38.źi ba mo	13.Śivā	7.źi ba mo
39.bdud rtsi mo	5.Amṛtā	8.bdud rtsi mo
40.zla ba	6.Rohiṇī	17.[lacking]
41.be chon(*sic*) mo	7.Daṇḍadhāriṇī	10.[illegible]
42.srin mo		11.srin mo ske gliṅ
43.za ba mo	10.Aśanā	12.z'a b'a mo
44.dga' ba mo	12.Rati	13.dg'a ba mo
45.gsod byed mo	9.Māraṇī	18.gsod byed ma
46.grub mo		15.grub mo
47.yid 'phrog ma	11.Vaśanā	14.yid 'phrog ma
48.gcig bur spyod ma	16.Kauverī	16.gcig bu spyod ma
49.rluṅ mo	14.Vāyavī	19.rluṅ mo
50.me mo	15.Āgneyī	20.mye mo
51.phag mo	17.Vārāhī	21.'phag mo
52.rgan byed ma	18.Cāmuṇḍā	22.drgan byad mo
53.sna chad mo	19.Chinnanāsā	23.[lacking]
54.chu lha mo	20.Vāruṇī	24.chu'i lha mo
55.nag mo chen mo	Cuckoo headed Aṅkuśī	25.khu byug
56.ra mgo dmar chen mo	Goat headed Pāśī	26.ra gdoṅ
57.bum sna sṅo nag	Lion headed Sphoṭā	27.seṅ gdoṅ
58.gsus 'dzin ser nag	Snake headed Ghaṇṭā	28.sbrul gdoṅ

The Sanskrit manuscript concerning Fifty-eight wrathful deities has not been discovered. Therefore, Sanskrit names of several deities are restored from Tibetan translation.

(1)।ཕྱུང་ནི་འཕྲིན་ལས་འདི་མན་ཆད་ཀྲོ་བོ་དཀྱིལ་འཁོར་བསྐྱེད།།འགྲོ་བ་འདུལ་བའི་དཀྱིལ་འཁོར་ཀྱིས་ཆུ་ཏུ་འབྱུང་བའི་འཕྲིན་ལས(1a2)་མཛད་དོ།།ཐམས་ཆད་དོ་བོ་མཐུམ་ཞིང་སྐུ།།བདེ་ཆེན་གར་དབང་སྐུ་གསུང་ཐུགས།།ཁྱི་བཟང་རྒྱུན་ཀྱི་འཁོར་ལོ་འི།།ཉི་ཀ་ལ་ཕྱག་འཚལ་ལོ།(1a3)སྐུ་འཕུལ་དུ་བའི་རྒྱུ་དག་ལས།སྷེ་འི་རྣལ་འབྱོར་བསྒོམ་པ་ཞིག།།སེམས་ཆན་ཡེ་ཤེས་བསྐྱེད་པའི་ཕྱིར།།ལེགས་པར(1a4)བཏགས་དེ་བསྟན་པར་བྱ།།སྟོབས་དཔོན་མཉེས་པར་མ་བྱས་ཤིག།།དབང་རྣམས་ཐོབ་པར་མ་བྱས་ན།།ཏུན་པ་ལས་སྩོགས་བཚོན་བ་(1a5)ནི་རྣམས།།འདས་བུ་ཅྱུང་ཅིང་བཀྲག་པར་འགྱུར།།ཡི་གེ་ཅྱིང་བཏགས་ཅྱིང་ཚོགས་ལ།།བསྟེན་པའི་ཚེག་གིས་རབ་མཚོན་ཏེ།།འཁོང་ནས་གབ་སྤྲུ་དོན་འབྲིན་དུ།།(1a6)སྟོན་པ་ཏོ་ཆེ་འི་ཐུགས་ལ།།གནས།།འདི་ནི་གསང་ཆེན་ཏེས་པ་འི།།འབྱས་བུ་ལམ་དུ་འགྱུར་པ་ཡིན།།རྒྱལ་བའི་དཀྱིལ་འཁོར་མ་ལུས་ལ།།འདི་ལས་གསང་བའི་ཏེས་དོན་ཆྱེད།།(1b1)ཀུན་གི་ཕྱག་རྒྱ་ཆེན་པོ་འི་མཚོག།།ཐོབས།།(sic)བསམས་བསྒོམས་ལ་རབ་སྦྱངས་བའི།།ཤེས་རབ་སྲན་བ་རྣམས་ཀྱིས་ཟུང་།།སྟོང་ཉུན་དང་ཚུལ་བཟང་ལ་བསྟན།།ལྱས་དང་འོང(1b2)སྟོང་གཏོང་ལ་སྟེག།།གཉན་དུ་ནམས་ཀྱང་སྟྱིན་ཀྲི་བྱ།།རྩོངས་དང་འཕྱུར་བས་གལ་ཏེ་ཕྱི།།དུས་ཅྱེད་པར་ཡང་སྲོག་ཟང་ཏེ།།བཞེགས་དང་བཞིབས་ལ་ཡུན་རིངས་གནས།།གང་(1b3)གིས་སྙང་ཆེན་ཚོས་འདུའི་སེམས།།མཐན་ལ་བཞག་པ་བཏུལ་ནས་སུ།།སྤྱགས་དང་ཕྱག་རྒྱ་རབ་བསྟན་ན།།དོས་འབྲུབ་ཡ་མཚན་ཆེན་པོར(1b4)འགྱུར།།རི་བོ་བསྐོར་བའི་སྟག་མ་དང།།མེན་ཏོག་འཕྲེང་བས་བརྒྱན་པ་ཡི།།དབེན་པའི་གནས་སུ་ཁྱད་པར་དུ།།འཛིན་པའི་སེམས་ཀྱིས་སྤྱག་(1b5)ལ་ཞི།།གདགས་ལས་ཕྱིད་གསུམ་གདུལ་ལྲ་དགང་རྒྱལ་ཆེན་པོ་བསྐྱེད་པའི་ཕྱིར།།སྐུ་འཕུལ་དུ་བའི་ཏིང་འཛིན་བསྒོམ།།

(2) །དེ་ཡན་ཆད་ཀྱིས་(1b6)འགྲོ་བོ་འི་དཀྱིལ་འཁོར་ཀྱི་ན་ཕྱི་ཀ་ཛོགས་ནས།།ལ་དང་པོར་མཐམ་པ་ཞིད་ཀྱི་ཏིད་ཏ་འཛིན་བསྒོ་བར་བྱ་སྟེ།ཆོས་ཐམས་ཆད་ཡེ་ནས་སྐྱེ་བ་དང།འགགས་པ་ཅྱེད་པའི་(2a1) །།དབྱིངས་ནས་སྐྱེ་བའི་ཚོ་འཕུལ་ཅེ་ལྟར་བསྟན་ན་ཡདག་དོན་དམ་པར་སྐྱེ་འགགས་ཅྱེད་པའི་དབྱིངས་ལས།།གཡོས་པ་རྩལ་ཚམ་ཡང་ཅྱེད་པར་བསམ་མོ།།དེ་ཡང་ཅེ་(2a2)མཛོན་ཞེ་ན།།རྒྱུང་ཆེན་པོ་དེ་ཉིད་ལས་འདི་སྐད་ཆེས་འབྱུང་ངོ་།།ཨེ་མ་ཧོ་

70

མཆོར་རྐྱད་ཀྱི་ཚོགས༔ཏྲོགས་པའི་སངས་རྒྱས་ཀུན་ཀྱིས་གསལ་བ༔སྐྱེ་བ་ཆེད་ལས་ཐབས་ཅད་སྐྱེ།།

(2a3)སྐྱེས་པ་ཞིད་ན་སྐྱེས་པ་ཆྱེད་ཞེས་བཙོད་པས།།ཐབང་ཅིག་མཐའ་བ་ཞིད་ཀྱི་ཏིང་ངེ་

འཛིན་བསྐོ་མོ།།

(3)ད་ནི་ཀུན་དུ་སྲུང་སྟེང་རྗེ་ཆེན་པོ་འི་ཏིང་ངེ་འཛིན་བསྐོམ་བར་བྱ་སྟེ།།འདི་སྐད་(2a4)

བཙོད་དོ།།སྐྱོང་པ་ཞིད་ལས་རབ་གསལ་བའི།།སྐྱིང་རྗེ་འི་ཡུས་ནི་བསྐོམ་བར་བྱ།།ཉིས་པ་ལས་

ནི་རྡོ་རྗེ་ཆེ།།མ་སུ་ཏུ་མན་ད་ལ་མ་ཞེས་བཙོད་པས།བདག་ཞིད་(2a5)མཐའ་པ་ཆེན་པོ་འི་

ཏིང་ངེ་འཛིན་བསྐོམ་བའི་དབྱིངས་ནས།།མ་ལས་ཉི་མའི་དཀྱིལ་འཁོར་སྐྱོང་།ཁམས་ཐབས་

ཅད།།དམར་ཕྱེམ་མེ་ཁྱབ་པར་བསྐོམ་མོ།།

(4)དེ་འི་(2a6)དབྱས་སུ་ཧཱུཾ་ཞེས་བཙོད་པས།།ཡི་གེ་ཧུམ་དམར་སྐུག་འབར་བ་གཅིག་གསལ་

བར་བསམས་སྟེ།།ཧུམ་སྔ་ར་ན་འཇ་ཞེས་བཙོད་པས།འོད་གཟེར་ཕྱོགས་བཅུར་འཕྲོས་པས།(2a

7)བདེ་བར་གཤེགས་པའི་ཐུགས་དམ་བསྐུལ།།འགྲོ་བ་རྒྱ་མཚོ་འི་དོན་བགྱིས་ནས།།སྨར་སང་

དུ་ར་ན་ཧུང་ཞེས་བཙོད་པས།།སྨར་སྨ་མའི་ཧུང་ལ་ཐིམ་སྟེ།ཧུང་དེ་ཐིམ་ཞེས་(2b1)ནུ་བས།།

བ་ཛྲ་ཏེ་སྨ་ཏེ་སྨ་བཙོད་པས།།རྡོ་རྗེ་ཙེ་ལྟ་བ་གཅིག་དུ་གྱུར་བར་བསམས་སྟེ།།

(5)ཨཱོ་འབྲུ་ཏ་ནི་རི་དེ་ཏུ་ཀ་ཧཱུཾ་ཞེས་བཙོད་པས། རྡོ་རྗེ་ལས་བདག་ཞིད་བཙཾ་ལྡན་(2b2)

འདས་འབྱུ་ཏ་དེ་རུ་ཀ་འབར་བ་ལྟ་ཆེན་པོ་གར་དགུ་དང་ལྡན་ག།ཞེགས་པོ་དཔའ་དའ་འོ་འཛིགས་

སུ་རུང་བའི་ཆ་བྱད་ཅན།།དགོང་པ་དངགའཞི་བ་དགའ་འཛིན་པར་བྱེད་པ་དང་སྐྱིང་རྗེ་ཆེན་(2

b3)པོ་དང་ཕྱིན་དུ་ཕྱམ་བ་དང་དོན་དས་པར་ཞི་བ་ཚོས་ཞིད་ཀྱི་སྐྱུ་ལས་མ་གསོལ་པས།།

འཇིག་རྟེན་ཆགས་འཇིག་གི་དུས་སྐྱར་དགུ་པ་གཅིག་གསལ་བར་བསྐོམས་སྟེ།།འདི་སྐད་

(2b4)ཅེས་བཙོད་དོ།།དེ་ལས་དཔལ་ཆེན་དེ་རུ་ཀ།།འབར་བ་ཆེན་པོ་འི་གར་དགུ་འི།།

འཇིགས་པ་འི་ནི་དུས་སྐྱར་དགྭར་ར་ཞེས་བཙོད་པས།ཡི་གེ་ར་ལེ་ནན་བྱུ་ཏུ་ཕྱིས་པ་(2b5)

ནི་མདོག་ལྟ་བུ་གཅིག་གསལ་བ་ལས།།

(6)ར་རག་ཏ་ར་རག་ཏ་ཞེས་བཙོད་པས།།རག་ལྟ་འི་ལ་སྟོང་འཕྲམ་ཡས་པ་གཅིག་དུ་བསྐོམ་

སྟེ།།ཏྲར་ཀྱི་ལ་ནི་སྟྲོ་ཏ་ཕྱིལ་སྟྲོ་འི་ལ་རྣབས་(2b6)ནུབ་དུ་ཕྱིལ།ནུབ་ཀྱི་ལ་རྣབས་བྱང་དུ་འཕྲོ་

བ་གཅིག་དུ་བསམས་སྟེ།།དེའི་དབྱས་སུ་ཀིང་ཀིང་ཞེས་བཙོད་པས།ཡི་གེ་ཀིང་དཀར་པོ་

གཅིག་ལས་གཏིང་དུས་གསར་རྗེང་ངེ་རབས་སྤྱར་(2b7)གྱུར་པའི་དབུས་སུ།།བ་ཞེས་བརྗོད་
པས།།ཡི་གེ་བ་མཐིང་ནག་ལས་འབད་འི་གཟལ་ཡས་ཁང་ཕྱི་དང་ནང་ཁྱེད་པ་ཀུན་དུ་ཡང་
ནང་དུ་གྱུར་པ་རྒྱ་ཕྱོགས་བཅུར་ཡོངས་སུ་མ་(3a1)ༀ།།ཆད་པ་གཅིག་གསལ་བར་བསམས་ཏེ
།།འི་ལ་འའི་སྐད་ཅེས་བརྗོད་པར་བྱའོ།།དུར་ཁྲོད་ཆེན་པོ་རབ་འཇིགས་པའི་ཁྲག་གི་ལ་སྒོང་
འཁྱུག་པའི་དཀྱིལ།།གཏིང་དུས་ཆེན་(3a2)པོའི་རི་རབ་ཀྱི།།སྟེང་ཀྱི་འབར་བའི་སྒྲོང་དཀྱིལ་ན།།
ཡེ་ཤེས་འབར་བའི་གཟལ་ཡས་ཁང་།།རྒྱ་ཡོངས་ཕྱོགས་བཅུར་མ་ཆད་པ།།ཕྱི་དང་ནང་ཁྱེད་
ཀུན་དུ་ནགའི་སྤྱར་གསལ་བ་དང་(3a3)གཟལ་ཁྱེད་ཁང་དེ་འི་དབུས་སམ།།
(7)འབྱང་བྲི་ཤུ་བྲི་ཤུད་དེ་ཞེས་བརྗོད་པས།།ཡེ་ཤེས་ཀྱི་ཐིག་བཞི་སྟེང་སྟེང་བཏབ་པ་ལས།།
འབར་བའི་འཁོར་ལོ་བརྩེགས་བཞི་དང་སྟུན་བའི་ཁྱམས་(3a4)གྲུ་བཞི་ལ་སྒོ་བཞི་འབར་བ་
ཆེན་པོའི་བར་ཁྱམས་གཉིས་དང་སྟུན་པ།།ཧོད་པ་དང་སྒྱལ་དང་གཉི་རྣ་དང་ཞིང་གསར་
རྗེང་ལས་བསྒོགས་པའི།།འཇིགས་བྱེད་ཆེན་པོའི་ཆ་(3a5)ལུགས་སྣ་ཚོགས་དང་སྟུན་ད།།
འབར་བའི་འཕྱེང་བ་མང་པོ་ཕྱོགས་བཅུ་ཀུན་དུ་འཁྱུགས་པ།།ཁར་ཕྱོགས་འཁོར་ལོའི་
བརྩེགས་ལ།།ཏྲི་ཟ་པོ་མོ་བསྒྱལ་བའི་སྟེང་དཀྱུ་མཆོག་གི་(3a6)སྤྱར་མོས་བསྣུས་པ།།སྲོ་ཕྱོགས་
ཀྱི་འཁོར་ལོའི་བརྩེགས་ལ།།གཔོ (sic)སྦྱིན་པོ་མོས་བསྒྱལ་བའི་སྟེང་དཀྱ་ཏེ་ཐབ་རྐྱུ་ར་
རེངས་ཀྱི་སྤྱར་མོར་བསྣུས་པ།།འུབ་ཕྱོགས་འཁོར་ལོའི་བརྩེགས་ལ།།(3a7)བྲིན་པོ་པོ་མོས་
བསྒྱལ་བའི་གདན་སྟེངས་ན།།གཟིག་ཀྱི་སྤྱར་མོས་བསྣུས་པ།།བྱང་ཕྱོགས་འཁོར་ལོའི་བརྩེགས་ལ
།།གཉིན་རྗེ་པོ་མོ་བསྒྱལ་བའི་གདན་སྟེངས་སུ།།སྤྱག་གི་སྤྱར་མོར་(3b1)བསྣུས་པར་བསམས་ཏེ
།།དེ་ཡང་རྒྱུད་ལས་འདི་སྐད་ཅེས་བརྗོད་པར་བྱ་དོ།།ༀ་འབར་བའི་འཁོར་ལོ་བརྩེགས་བཞི་པ།།
གྲུ་ཆད་བཞི་ཡིས་རྣམ་པར་བརྒྱན།།གྲུ་བཞི་སྒོ་ཁྱུད་བཞི་དང་(3b2)ལྷུན།།འབར་བའི་བར་
ཁྱམས་གཉིས་གིས་མཛེས།།ཧོད་སྒྱལ་སྣ་ཚོགས་གཉི་རྣར་བརྗེད།།འབར་བའི་འཕྱེང་བ་མང་པོ
འཁྱུག།ཁྱུ་མཆོག་མ་དེ་གཟིག་དང་སྤྱག།གདུམ་བ་(3b3)ནི་དོམ་ཀྱི་སྤྱར་བས་ནེ།།དབང་ཕྱུག་
སྤ་ཆེན་ལས་བསྒོགས་གཟུང་།
(8)∴།དེ་སྤྱར་གསལ་བ་དགའ་བདག་ཞེད་དུས་གསུམ་ཀྱི་དེ་བཞིན་གཤེགས་པ་ཐམས་ཅད་ཀྱི་
རྒྱ་གསུང་ཐུགས་རྡོ་རྗེ་(3b4)འི་བདག་ཞེད་ཀུང་ཡིན་ལ།།སྲོ་པོ་རྒྱལ་པོ་ཡང་ཡིན་མོད་ཀྱི

དོན་དམ་པར་ཆོས་ཉིད་མཉམ་པ་ཉིད་ལས་མ་གཡོས་པའི་དབྱིངས་ནས་ཁེན་དུ་དགྱེས་པའི་
གཉིས་མེད་ངས་ཀྱིས(3b5)ཏེ་དེ་ཞེས་བརྗོད་པས།ཡུམ་གྲོ་ཏེ་ནུ་རེ་རྒྱན་དང་ཆ་ལུགས་གཙོ་བོ་
དང་མཚུན་པ་ལ།།དཔུ་རྒྱན་སྤྱེད་པ་ཅིག་གཡོན་ཕྱོགས་སུ་ཞིང་སྟོལ་མའི་གདན་སྟེངས་སུ་
བཞུགས་པ་ལ།(3b6)འཇརྟཱུྃ་པང་དོ་ཞེས་བརྗོད་པས།མ་ཆགས་པའི་ཏིང་ངེ་འཛིན་ལས།
ཆགས་པའི་ཡིད་གཡོས་པར་བསམས་སྟེ།།འཇང་ལྷགས་ཀྱུས་ནི་བཟུང་ཤུང་ཞགས་པས་ནི་འཁྱིལ་
།པས་(3b7)ལྷགས་སྦྱོག་ཀྱིས་བསྣམས།།ཏོ་དྲིལ་བུས་དགྱེས་པར་བསྐྱོད་པས།།ཤུང་རྒྱབ་ཀྱི་
སེམས་ཡུམ་གྱི་མཁའ་ལ་བབ་སྟེ།འདི་སྐད་ཅེས་བརྗོད་པར་བྱ་གོ།།བདག་ཉིད་སངས་རྒྱས(4a
1)༡༽།།ཐམས་ཅད་ཀྱི་སྐུ་གསུང་ཐུགས་ཀྱི་རོ་རྗེ་བདག་ཁྲོ་རྒྱལ་ཡེ་ནས་ཡིན་པའི་ཕྱིར།།དེ་
བཞིན་ཉིད་ཀྱི་དབྱིངས་ནས་ནི།།ཁྲོ་མོ་དབང་ཕྱུག་མཆོན་བྱུང་སྟེ།།དེ་ནི་དགྱེས་པའི་(4a2)
གཉིས་མེད་ངས་ཀྱིས།།རིན་ཆེན་པད་མས་རྒྱལ་མཆོག་ནས།།གཉིས་སྤྱེད་དགྱེས་པའི་འཁྲིལ་པ་སྟེ།།
བྱང་རྒྱབ་སེམས་སྟྲེན་དགའ་པ་ལས།།ཧཱུྃ་བྲི་ནྲྀ་གྲོ་ཏེ་ཧ་མ་མན་འཛ་ལའཔཏ་པཏ་ཏུ་(4a3)ལ་
ཧུ་ལ་ཞེས་བརྗོད་པས།།བྱང་ཆུབ་ཀྱི་སེམས་དེ་ལས་འོད་ཟེར་ཕྱོགས་བཅུར་ཕྱུ་ཀྱིས་འཕྲོས་པས།
།འཇིག་རྟེན་དྲུག་གི་ཕྱོགས་བཅུ་ཐམས་ཅད།།ཁྲོ་བོ་ཆེན་པོ་ཞིག་གི་(4a4)ཧྱལ་སྟེང་ལ་མཆོན་
ཆ་ཡང་ཞིང་གི་རྡུལ་སྟེང་ཕོགས་པའི་སྟྲག་ཀྱིས་ལྷག་ཀྱིས་གང་བར་བསམས་སྟེ།།
(9)ཤར་ཕྱོགས་ནས་ནཱ་ཛ་ཏུ་ཀ་གང་འག་སྐྱུང་ཀྱི་བྲེ་མ་ཚམ་འཐོན་བར་(4a5)བསམ་མོ།།
ཫྙོ་ཕྱོགས་ནས་ནད་ན་དེ་ཛ་ཀ་གང་འག་སྐྱུང་ཀྱི་བྲེ་མ་ཚམ་འཐོན་བར་བསམ་མོ།།ནུབ་ཕྱོགས་
ནས་ནད་ཨ་དེ་ཛ་ཀ་གང་འག་སྐྱུང་ཀྱི་བྲེ་མ་ཚམ་འཐོན་བར་བསམ་མོ།།(4a6)བྱང་ཕྱོགས་
ནས་ཀར་ཨ་དེ་ཛ་ཀ་གང་འག་སྐྱུང་ཀྱི་བྲེ་མ་ཚམ་འཐོན་བར་བསམ་སྟེ།།ལ་འདི་སྐྱ་ཅེས་
བརྗོད་པར་བྱགོ།འཇིག་རྟེན་དྲུག་གི་ཕྱོགས་བཅུ་དག་མ་སྣ་ཡས་ཁྱབ་(4a7)པར་འགྲོ་བ་ཱི།།
དགྱལ་འགྱར་སྟྱོང་གསུམ་འཇིག་རྟེན་ཚམ།ཧྱལ་སྟེང་ཕྱོགས་བཅུར་འཐོན་བར་འགྱུར་ཏེ།
ནས་བཙམ་ལྱན་འདས་དགྱེས་ཆེན་པོ་ྦུ་དང་ཕྱག་ཞབས་སྟོང་ཁམས་(4b1)ཀྱི་ཧྱལ་སྟེང་
ལ།།མཆོན་ཆ་ཡང་ཞིང་ཀྱི་ཧྱལ་སྟེང་འཛིན་པ་དེ་དག་ཐམས་ཅག་དབང་བྱུང་ཆེན་པོ་དང་
དུར་ཁྲོག་ཀྱི་བདག་པོ་དགཱིགས་པ་ཆེན་པོ་ལས་བསྒྱོགས་སྟེ།།ཁུ་ཤུལ་ཀྱི་(4b2)གདན་ལ་
བཀྱང་སྐྱམ་ཀྱི་ཆུལ་དུ་བཞུགས་པར་བསམ།།ཏེ་འདི་སྐད་ཅེས་བརྗོད་པར་བྱགོ།དེ་ནས་

བཙོམ་ལྡན་དགྱེས་ཆེན་པོ།དཔལ་དང་ཕྱག་ཞབས་སྟོང་ཁམས་ཀྱི།ཧྲུལ་སྟེང་(4b3)མཆོན་ཆ་
འཛིན་པ་དེ।དབང་ཕྱུག་ཆེ་དང་དུར་བོད་ཀྱི།བདག་པོ་དྲེགས་པ་ཆེན་པོ་ཚོ།ཤུག་ཀྱི་གདན་
ལ་བཀྱུང་བསྐྱམ་ཆུལ་དུ།བཞུགས།དེ་དག་ཐམས་ཅད་ཀུན་ཀུན་འཛིགས།(4b4)བྱེད་ཆེན་
པོའི་ཆ་ལུགས་དང་ཧྲས་བའི་ང་རོས་སྐྲག་པའི་སྒྱེ།དཔུང་འབར་བའི་དཀྱིལ་ན།གདུ་གསུམ་
ཕྱག་དྲུག་ཞབས་བཞིར་གྱུར་ད་ནས།ཌི་ཟ་དང་གཚོད་སྩྲིད་(4b5)དང་སྟིན་པོ་དང་གཤིན་རྗེ་
ལས་བསྟོགས་པ།ཕོ་མོ་བསྩོལ་པའི་གདན་སྟེང་ན།བཀྱུང་བསྐྱམ་གྱི་ཚུལ་དུ་བཞུགས་པར་
བསམ་མོ།།དེ་ལ་འདི་སྐྲད་ཆེས་བཙོད་པར་བྱ་འོ།།(4b6)དེ་ཀུན་འཛིགས་བྱེད་ཆེན་པོ་ཡི།ཆ
ལུགས་ཪམ་བའི་ང་རོ་ཡིས།།འབར་བའི་སྐྲོང་ན་དུ་གསུམ་པ།ཕྱག་དྲུག་ཞབས་བཞི་དི་ཟ་
དང་གཚོད་སྟིན་ཧྲིན་པོ་(4b7)གཤིན་རྗེ་ལས་བསྟོགས་པའི་ཁྲི་ཤུག་ཀྱི་གདན་ལ་བཀྱུང་སྐྱམ་
དུ་བཞུགས།།ཕོ་མོ་སྟིན་ཕྱུང་ཀྱི་ཚོགས་དེ་དག་ཐམས་ཅད་ཀུན།།ཤར་ཕྱོགས་འདག་འདག་སྒྱུ་ཀྱི་
བྱེ་མ་(5a1)༠།།སྟེད་སྩོན་རྡོར་བ།དབཔལ་བྲག་འབྱུང་ནོ་རྗེ་བཛྲ་ཧི་དུ་ཀར་སྩུད་པར་བསམ་མོ།།སྩོ་
ཕྱོགས་འགྲོ་པོ་འབག་འབག་སྩུང་ཀྱི་བྱེ་མ་སྟེད་འཐོན་དཀྱདཔལ་འབག་ཐུང་རིན་པོ་ཆེ་དཀ་རང་(5a
2)ན་ཧི་ཪུ་ཀར་གྱུར་པར་བསམ་མོ།།ནུབ་ཕྱོགས་འགྲོ་པོ་འབག་འབག་སྩུང་ཀྱི་བྱེ་མ་སྟེད་རྡོར་དཔ།
དཔལ་འབག་ཐུང་པད་མ་ཧི་ཪུ་ཀར་གྱུར་པར་བསམ་མོ།།བྱང་ཕྱོགས་ཀྱི་འགྲོ་པོ་གང་(5a3)
འབག་སྩུང་གི་བྱེ་མ་སྟེད་སྩོན་དཀ་དཔལ་འབག་ཐུང་ལས་ཀྱི་རིགས་ཀར་མ་ཧི་ཪུ་ཀར་གྱུར་པར་
བསམ་སྟེ།།
(10)དེ་ལ་འདི་སྐྲད་ཆེས་བཙོད་པར་བྱའོ།།ཁྲི་པོ་སྟིན་ཕུང་དེ་ཀུན་ཡབ་དཔལ།(5a4)ནི་ཁྲག
ཐུང་རོ་རྗེ་དག་རིན་པོ་ཆེ་དང་པད་མ་ཡབདཔལས་སུ་གྱུར་དེ་ཕྱོགས་བཞིར་བཞུགས།།བཙུན་
མོ་ཁྲག་ཐུང་ཆེན་མོ་འི་རྣམས།།ས་འི་རྒྱལ་འཁྲིལ་ཏེ་(5a5)བཞུགས།།ཕྱོ་ཏེ་ནུ་རི་འཇ་ཏུ་
པམ་ཏོ་ཞིས་བཙོད་པས།།ཁྲི་པོ་གཙོ་པོ་སོ་སོ་འི་ཡུམ་བའི་དང་གཡོན་ཕྱོགས་སུ་འཁྲིལ་པར་བ
སམ་མོ།།
(11)དེ་ནས་ཡབ་ཡུམ་གཉིས་སུ་སྩེད་པའི་བྱང་(5a6)ཆུབ་ཀྱི་སེམས་དགྱེས་པའི་ཕི་སྟིན་ལས།
ཀྲི་ཀྲི་ཀྲི་ཀྲི་ཀྲི་ཀྲི་ཀྲ་བཙོད་པས།དཀར་མོའི་ཚོགས་དང།།ཀྲུན་མོའི་ཚོགས་དང།སྤྱོས་མོའི་

ཚོགས་དང་།།གདུམ་མོའི་ཚོགས་(5a7)དང་སྐྱེ་བ་ཅན་གྱི་ཚོགས་དང་རབ་ཀྲོངས་མའི་ཚོགས་
དང་།།ཐལ་བྱེད་མའི་ཚོགས་ལས་བསྐྱིགས་པ་རྣམས་།།ཞིང་ཁྱུང་པའི་གདན་སྟེངས་ན།།འབར་
བའི་འཁོར་ལོའི་(5b1)ཕར་མཚམས་ནས་།།ཧྣ་བའི་མདངས་ཀྱིས་བསྐོར་ཏེ་བཞུགས་པར་
བསམ་མོ།།དེ་ལ་འདི་སྐྱད་ཅེས་བརྗོད་པར་བྱ་འོ།།དེ་ནས་དགྱེས་ཏེ་དུ་བརྗོད་པས།།བྱང་ཆུབ་
སེམས་སྤྱིན་(5b2)དག་པ་ལས།།གཀར་མོའི་ཚོགས་དང་ཀྱུན་མོའི་ཚོགས་ལྷོས་མོའི་ཚོགས་དང་
།།གདུམ་མོའི་ཚོགས།།སྐྱེ་བ་ཅན་དང་མང་ཚོགས་རྣམས།།ཚོགས་རྣམས་རང་གི་(5b3)ལག་ཆ་
དང་།།མཚར་ཆས་ནས་ཧྣ་བཏོན་ཏེ།།འབར་ཅེན་འཁོར་ལོའི་ཕར་མཚམས་ནས་འཁོར་
བར་ཧྣ་བའི་མདངས་ཀྱིས་འཁོད།།

(12)དེ་ནས་ཡབ་ཡུམ་གཉིས་(5b4)སུ་ཆྱེད་པའི་བྱང་ཆུབ་ཀྱི་སེམས་ཀྱི་སྟྲིན་ལས།།དེ་དེ་
དེ་དེ་དེ་དེ་དེ།ཞེས་བརྗོད་པས།།སེན་གདོང་ཅེན་མོའི་ཚོགས་དང་།།སྤྱག་གདོང་ཅེན་མོའི་
ཚོགས་དང་(5b5)ལྱ་གདོང་ཅེན་མོའི་ཚོགས་དང་།།ཁྱི་གདོང་ཅེན་མོའི་ཚོགས་དང་།།གཞད་
གདོང་ཅེན་མོ་འི་ཚོགས་དང་།།གཀང་ཀ་གདོང་ཅེན་མོའི་ཚོགས་དང་།།དུར་བྱ་གདོང་ཅེན་མོ་འི་
(5b6)ཚོགས་དང་།།བྱ་རོག་གདོང་ཅེན་མོའི་ཚོགས་དང་།།འུག་གདོང་ཅེན་མོའི་ཚོགས་ལས་
བསྐྱིགས་པ་རྣམས།།ཞིང་ཁྱུང་པའི་གདན་སྟེངས་ན།།འཇིགས་ཚུལ་ནྣོ་བ་སྐ་ཚོགས་(5b7)ཀྱིས་
བརྒྱན་ཏེ།།འབར་བའི་འཁོར་ལོའི་ཕྱི་རོལ་གྱི།།ཕར་ཕྱོགས་ཀྱི་མཚམས་ནས།།ཉིན་དུ་འཇིགས་
པའི་མདངས་ཀྱིས་བསྐོར་ཏེ།།བཞུགས་པར་བསམ་མོ།།དེ་ལ་འདི་སྐྱད་(6a1)༡།།ཅེས་བརྗོད་
པར་བྱའོ།།དེ་ནས་དགྱེས་ཏེ་དེ་དེ་བརྗོད་པས།།བྱང་ཆུབ་སེམས་སྤྱིན་དག་ལས།།སེན་གདོང་ཅེན་
མོའི་ཚོགས་དང་ནི།།སྤྱག་དང་ལ་དང་ཁྱི་དང་གཞན།།གང་ཀ་(6a2)དུར་བྱ་འུག་གདོང་ཅེ།།
ཚོགས་རྣམས་རང་གི་ལག་ཆ་དང་།།མཚར་ཆས་ནས་འཇིགས་བཏོན་སྟེ།།འབར་བའི་འཁོར་
ལོའི་ཕྱི་རོལ་གྱི།།ཕར་གི་ཕྱོགས་ཀྱི་མཚམས་དག་(6a3)ནས་འཁོར་བར་འཇིགས་པའི་
མདངས་ཀྱིས་འཁོད།།

(13)དེ་ནས་བཅོམ་ལྡན་འདས་དགྱེས་པ་ཅེན་པོ་ཡབ་ཡུམ་གཉིས་སུ་ཆྱེད་པའི་བྱང་ཆུབ་
སེམས་དགྱེས་པའི་སྟྲིན་ལས།།ཐཏ་ཐཏ་(6a4)ཐཏ་ཐཏ་ཞེས་བརྗོད་པས།།རྗེ་རྗེ་བསྙེངས་འགྲོ་
མ་འི་ཚོགས་དང་གདོང་མའི་ཚོགས་དང་འཇིགས་ཏྗེན་མའི་ཚོགས་དང་(6a5)རོ་ལངས་

མའི་ཚོགས་ལས་བསྐྱགས་པ་རྣམས་ཞིང་རྒྱུང་པའི་གདན་སྟེངས་ན་རང་གི་ལག་ཆ་དང་།
བཅས་ནས་དཀྱིལ་འཁོར་(6a6)སྒྲོ་བཞིར་ངམ་པའི་གཟུགས་ཀྱིས་འཁོད་པར་བསམས་ཏེ།།
འདི་སྐད་ཅེས་བརྗོད་པར་བྱའོ།།དེ་ནས་དགྱེས་དེ་ཕྱད་བརྗོད་(6a6)པས།།བྱུང་རྒྱབ་སེམས་
 སྟིན་དག་པ་ལས།།རྟོ་རྗེ་བསྙེང་འགྲོ་གདོང་མོ་དག།།འཇིག་རྟེན་མ་དང་ཐབས་བྱེད་མ།(6b1)
ཚོགས་རྣམས་རང་གི་ལག་ཅ་དདག་ཏོ་མཆོར་བཅས་ནས་ཐམ་བཏོན་དེ།།དཀྱིལ་འཁོར་སྒྲོ་
བཞིར་ངམ་གཟུགས་གནས།།
(14)དེ་ནས་(6b2)ཡབ་ཡུམ་གཉིས་སུ་སྤྱེད་པའི་བྱང་རྒྱབ་སེམས་ཆ་དགྱེས་པའི་སྟིན་ལས།།
ཕད་ཅེས་བརྗོད་པ་ལས།།ཁྲོ་བོ་སྟིན་ཕུང་གི་ཚོགས་དེ་དག་ཐམས་ཅད།(6b3)གནག་ཀོང་
འདྲོགས་པ་འདྲ་བའི་ཆུལ་དུ་ཤེན་དུ་འབྲོས་པར་བསམ་མོ།།
(15)དེ་ནས་བདག་ཉིད་སྐུན་གྱིས་གྲུབ་པར་བྱ་ཞིག།དུས་གསུམ་གི་(6b4)བདེན་བར་གཤེགས་
པའི་སྐུ་གསུང་ཐུགས་དང་མཉམ་བར་སྤྱུར་དགོས་པའི་ཕྱིར།།བདག་ནི་བྱ་བྱེད་གི་རང་བཞིན།།
ཡུ་ནི་ཁ་ཚ་མའི་(6b5)རང་བཞིན་དུ་བསམས་སྟེ།།འདི་སྐད་ཅེས་བརྗོད་པར་བྱོ།།དགྱེས་
པའི་སྟིན་ལས་ཕྱོགས་བཅུར་ཏེ།།ཕད་ཅེས་བསྒྲགས་པས་ཐམས་(6b6)ཅད་འགྲོས།།དེ་ནས་
དཔལ་ཆེན་ཁྲོ་བོའི་རིགས།།སྤྲུ་གིས་གྲུབ་པར་བྱ་བའི་ཕྱིར།།རང་གི་ངང་ཆུལ་དེ་བཟུངས་ནས
།།སྐྱལ་ཆིག་(6b7)འདི་དག་རར་དུ་བརྗོད།།བྱུང་སྟོན་གི་ཐུགས་དས་ཆེན་པོ་ནི།།འཇིག་རྟེན་
མ་ལུས་ཐམས་ཅད་ཀུན།།རྒྱལ་པའི་ཞིང་དུ་སྤྱུར་བའི་ཕྱིར་དུ་(7a1)ༀ།།སྐུ་ནི་དབྱིག་དུ་བདག
བསྐྱེད་ཅིག་ཅེས་བརྗོད་པས།།ཡབ་ཡུམ་གཉིས་སུ་སྤྱེད་པའི་བྱང་རྒྱབ་གྱི་སེམས་ལས།།ཡེ་ཤེས་
གི་འོད་ཟེར་ལས་(7a2)བདག་གི་ལུས་ངག་ཡིད་གསུ་གི་རྟོག་པ་སྤྲངས།།བྱང་རྒྱབ་ཀྱི་སེམས་
གསེར་ཞུན་མ་ལྟ་འཁྱུར་འགྱུར་དེ།ༀ་ༀ་ཧཱུ་ཞེས་བརྗོད་པས་(7a3)ཡེ་གེ་ༀ་དང་ༀ་དང་ཧཱུ་
དང་གསུ་ལས་ལུ་ག་རྒྱུད་ཀྱི་ཆུལ་དུ་སྟེངས་པས།བདག་གི་ཕྱགས་གར་ཕེམ་ཕྱགས་ཀ་ནས་རོ་
རྗེ་ལམ་དུ་འབྱུང་སྟེ།(7a4)ཕྱམ་གི་མ་ཏྲ་ལ་ཕེམ་ནས་ཆོས་ཉིད་བྱང་རྒྱབ་ཀྱི་སེམས་ཀྱི་རང་
བཞིན་དུ་གྱུར་དེ།དེ་ལ་དབྱིངས་ནས་སྟ་བོ་སོའི་ཕྱགས་དང་སྣྱིང་པོ་ལས་(7a5)བསྐྱགས་པ་
འབྱུང་བར་བསམས་སྟེ།འདི་སྐད་ཅེས་བརྗོད་པར་བྱོ།ཐབས་དང་ཤེས་རབ་གཉིས་སྤྱེད་པའི་
ཡེ་ཤེས་ཟེར་གིས་ལུས་རྟོག་སྤངས།(7a6)གསེར་ཞུན་ལྟ་ཕུ་འི་སེམས་དག་ལས།།གསུམ་གི་བྱེན་

རྣབས་འོད་ཀྱིས་འགྲོ་ཁྲུགས་ཀར་ཐིམ་ནས་སྐུ་འི་དཀྱིལ་རྟོ་རྗེ་ལས་འབྱུང་ཡུམ་གི་(7a7)མཐྭ། ཚོམ་སྐུ་བྱང་རྒྱབ་སེམས་སུ་གནས་ལ་རྣམས་སོ་སོ་འི་སྟེང་པོ་འི་སྒྱུད་དེ་ནས་འགྲོ་འདུ་འི་སྐྱར་སྒྱོ་བསྒྲས་ཕྱག་རྒྱ་ཆེན་པོ་འི་སྐུ་(7b1)གཉིས་རྫོགས།།

(16)ཐབས་ཀྱི་ཕྱག་རྒྱར་གྱུར་ད་པའི་ཕྱིར།།ཨིཿམ་ད་ཧུ་ནུ་ཏེ་གཉན་ན་བ་རྗེ་ས་ཧྲ་བྲ་ཨད་མ་གོ་ཧྨ་སྟོང་པ་ཆེན་པོ་དེ་ཁོ་ན་ཉིད་(7b2)ཀྱི་བདག་ཉིད་ཆེན་པོ་ཡང་དགོ།ཨིཿམ་ད་ཨླ་ཏ་རེ་ཁ་གཉན་ན་བ་རྗེ་ས་ཧྲ་བ་ཨད་མ་གོི་ཧྨ་ཀྱི་སྦོང་ལྥ་ཙུ་འི་ཡེ་ཤེས་(7b3)ཆེན་པོ་ཡང་ང་དགོ།ཨིཿམ་ད་པྱད་ཏ་པྱ་བེ་ཁ་གཉན་ན་བ་རྗེ་ར་ས་ཧྲ་བ་ཨད་མོ་གོི་ཧྨ་མཐམ་ཉ་བ་ཉིད་ཀྱི་ཡེ་ཤེས་ཆེན་(7b4)པོ་ཡང་ང་དགོ།ཨིཿམ་ད་ས་མན་ཏ་གཉན་ན་བ་རྗེ་ས་ཧྲ་བྲ་ཨད་མ་གོི་ཧྨ་གཤོ་སོ་ཀྱུན་ད་རྟོགས་པའི་ཡེ་ཤེས་ཆེན་པོ་(7b5)ཡང་དགོ།ཨིཿམ་ད་ཀྱིད་ཏ་ཨ་ནུ་ལྥ་ན་གཉན་ན་བ་རྗེ་ས་ཧྲ་བྲ་ཨད་མ་གོི་ཧྨ།།ཐུ་བའ་ནན་ཏན་བསྒྲུབ་པའི་ཡེ་ཤེས་ཆེན་པོ་ཡང་དགོ།(7b6)ཨིཿམ་ད་ས་ནྲ་ཏ་ཐ་གཱ་ཏ་ཀ་ཡ་ཱ་བ་རྗེ་ས་ཧྲ་བྲ་ཨད་མ་གོི་ཧྨ།དེ་བཞིན་གཤེགས་པ་ཐམས་ཅད་ཀྱི་སྐུ་རྟོ་རྗེ་འི་བདག་ཉིད་ཆེན་པོ་ཡང་དགོ།(7b7)ཨིཿས་ནྲ་ཏ་ཐ་ག་ཏ་བག་བཛྲ་ས་ཧྲ་བྲ་ཨད་མ་གོི་ཧྨ་དེ་བཞིན་གཤེགས་པ་ཐམས་ཅད་ཀྱི་གསུང་རྟོ་རྗེ་འི་བདག་ཉིད་ཐ་ཡང་དགོ།ཨིཿས་ནྲ་(8a1)༈།།སུ་ག་ཏ་ཀ་སྲ་གཱར་ཏ་ཙིཏ་ཏ་བ་རྗེ་ས་ཧྲ་བྲ་ཨད་མ་གོི་ཧྨ་དེ་བཞིན་གཤེགས་པ་ཐམས་ཅད་ཀྱི་ཐུགས་རྟོ་རྗེ་འི་བདག་ཉིད་ཡང་ང་དགོ།(8a2)ཨིཿས་ནྲ་ཏ་ཐ་གཱ་ཏ་ཨ་ནུ་ར་གཱ་ན་ས་ཧྲ་བྲ་ཨད་མ་གོི་ཧྨ་དེ་བཞིན་གཤེགས་པ་ཐམས་ཅད་ཀྱི་ཡུམ་གི་ཆགས་པ་འི་རྟོ་པོ་འི་བདག་ཉིད་ཡང་ང་དགོ།(8a3)ཨིཿས་ནྲ་ཏ་ཐ་གཱ་ཏ་པྱ་ཙ་མེ་གཱ་ས་ཧྲ་བྲ་ཨད་མ་གོི་ཧྨ་དེ་བཞིན་གཤེགས་པ་ཐམས་ཅད་ཀྱི་མཆོད་པ་ཆེན་པོ་འི་བདག་ཉིད་ཆེན་པོ་ཡང་ང་དགོ།།

(8a4)(17)དེ་ཡན་ཅད་རྒྱལ་བའི་སྲས་སུ་བདག་བསྐྱེད་པ་འོ།དེ་ལྟར་ཡེ་ཤེས་ལྷ་འི་རང་བཞིན་དུ་ང་རྒྱལ་བསྐྱེད་ནས་ཤད་ནི་འདི་མན་ཅད་བདག་(8a5)ཀྱི་སྲས་སུ་རྒྱལ་བྲ་བསྐྱེད་པར་བྱ་སྟེ་དེ་ཡང་ཡབ་ཀྱི་རྟོ་རྗེ་རྩེ་ལྥ་པ་འི་སྟེང་དུ་ཡི་གེ་གཆིག་བསྒོམ་ཡུམ་གི་མཆ་ལ་བབ་མ་འདམ་བརྒྱད་(8a6)ཀྱི་སྟེང་དུམ་ལས་ནི་མ་འི་དཀྱིལ་འཁོར་དུ་བསམས་སྟེ་འཛའ་ཧཱུྃ་པམ་རྟོ་ཞིས་བརྗོད་པས།ཡབ་ཀྱི་ཕྱག་རྒྱ་ལྷགས་ཀྱིས་བཟུངས།ཞགས་(8a7)པས་བཅིངས།

ལྷ་གས་སློ་ག་ཀྱིས་བསྒམས་དྲིལ་བུས་དགྱེས་པར་བསྐྱོང་ནས་ཆུང་ཀྱུབ་ཀྱི་སེམས་ཡུམ་གི་མཚ་
ལ་བསམས་སྟེ་དི་ལ་འདི་(8b1)འདི་སྐད་ཅེས་བརྗོད་པར་བྱ་དྒཱ་རྡྷཱ་རྗེ་པད་མོ་ར་ཏྲིན་རྟབས་
པས།།ཏུྃ་ལས་རྡོ་རྗེ་རྗེ་ཤྲ་ལྥ་པ་བ་ལས་པད་མར་གྱུར་པའི་དབུས།(8b2)མ་ལས་ཉི་མའི་དྐྱིལ་
འཁོར་བསམ།།ཧུང་ད་ཡ་ལས་བསྐྱགས་པ་ཡེ་ཤེ་བསྐྱལ་བ་འདི་དྒ་ཆུལ་བཞིན་བྱ།།དི་ལྟར་
བརྗོད་(8b3)པ་དང་།ཡུམ་གི་གསང་བའི་གནས་བཞིར་བསྟེན་པའི་ཡན་ལག་ལ་བཞི་དགོང་
པར་བྱ་སྟེ།།འདི་སྐད་ཅེས་བརྗོད་པར་བྱའོ།།(8b4)བསྟེན་པ་དང་ནི་ཉེ་བསྟེན་པོ།།བསྒྲུབ་པ་
དང་ནི་བསྒྲུབ་ཆེན་པོ།།ཕྱི་ཀྱི་པད་མའི་དྐྱིལ་འཁོར་དུ།།པདེ་བ་ཕྱགས་ཀྱི་དྐྱིལ་(8b5)
འཁོར་སློབ།།

(18)མཐས་རྒྱས་ཕྲིན་ཚོགས་མ་ལུས་ལ་དྐྱིས་མཐམ་མཆོག་གི་ཕྲིན་བས་ཐིག་འདི་ལས་དྐྱིལ་
འཁོར་གསང་བར་(8b6)བཀོད།།ཞྲི་ཧ་ཕྲི་ཤུད་དེ་ཞེས་བརྗོད་པས།གོང་དུ་བསྐྱེད་པའི་
རག་ཏ་འི་ལྷ་སློང་དྐོང་ཊུས་ཀྱི་རི་རབ་དང་།

རྣན་རྲ་འི་གཞལ་ཡས་ཁང་དུ་(9a1)༣།།གནས་ལྷགས་ལྲུགས་ཡུར་མོང་འབར་བའི་གཞེར་དང་།།
འབར་བའི་འཁོར་ལོ་དང་ཞིང་བསྐྱལ་མའི་གནན་ཁྲི་དང་འབར་བའི་སྐ་འབྲར་དང་ཀྲུ་ཆད་
དང་(9a2)འབར་བའི་པར་ཁྱམས་གཉིས་དང་སྐྲོ་བའི་ནི་སྐོ་ཁྱང་དང་།སྤུལ་དང་ཐོད་ཕྲེང་
ཀྱིས་བཀྱན་པའི་དྲུས་སྲུ།།

(19)ཨཱོྃ་འབྱུ་ད་བྱེ་ཏེ་ཏུ་ཀ་(9a3)མ་ཏུ་ཚན་ཏ་ས་ན་དུས་སྲུན་ད་ཀ་ཏུ་ན་པ་ཙ་ཏུྃ་པད་ཆེས་
བརྗོད་པས།།དྐྱིལ་འཁོར་ཀྱི་ཕྲེ་བའི་དྲུས་སུ་བདུད་མ་དང་རུ་དྲ་པོ་མོ་(9a4)བསྒྲལ་བའི་
གདན་སྟེངས་སུ།།བཙ་ཝན་འདས་འབྱུ་ད་ཧེ་དུ་ཀ།ཀུ་མཁྱ་མཚོག་སྲུག་གནགས།།འབྱུ་གསུ་ཤུག་དུག
ལ།གཡས་དང་པོ་ན་(9a5)སློང་འགྱི་འཇིག་རྟེན་འཁོར་ཡུག་དུ་བཅས་པ་བར་མ་ན་རྡོ་རྗེ།
ཐ་མ་ནི་ཡེ་ཤེས་ཀྱི་གཙོག།།གཡོན་དང་པོ་ན་དག་སྡབར་མ་ན་(9a6)རལ་གི་(sic)།མཐ་མ་
ན་ཡེ་ཤེས་ཀྱི་གཙོག།།སྐལ་པའི་མྱེ་དྤང་གི་དྐྱིལ་ན་སྦུལ་དང་ཐོད་འཕྱང་གིས་སྐྱ་ལ་བརྒྱན་
ཅིང་།།(9a7)འཇིགས་ཆུལ་རྣམ་པ་སྣ་ཚོགས་དང་ཕྲན་ཏེ།ཡུམ་ཀྲོ་ཏེ་ཤྲ་རི་ཡདབཀྲྱན་དང་ཆ་
ལུགས་གཙོ་པོ་དང་མཐུན་(9b1)པ་གཡོན་འཕྱོགས་སུ་འཁྲིལ་བར་བསམ་མོ།

(20)།།ཨོཾ་བ་ཛྲ་མ་ཏུ་ཕྲི་ཏེ་ར་ཀྵ་ས་དུས་སྟྲན་ད་ཀ་ཏུ་ན་པ་ཙ་ཧཱུྃ་ཕཊ་ཨོཾ་བ་ཛྲ་(9b2)དར་མ་གྲོ་ཏེ་ཤྲ་རེ་ཧཱུྃ་ཕཊ་ཅེས་བརྗོད་པས།ཕར་ཕྱོགས་འཁོར་ལོ་འི་རྩིབས་ལ་ཨཱ་ཱི་ཨ་པོ་མོ་བསྐོལ་བའི་གདན་སྟེངས་སུ་ཕྱུང་མཆོག་(9b3)ཀྱི་སྦྱར་མོས་བསྒུས་པའི་གདན་སྟེངས་སུ་བདག་ཉིད་བཙོམ་ལྡན་འདས་བ་ཛྲ་ཕྲི་ཏེ་ར་ཀཱ་སྨ་མདོག་སྟོ་གནག་གདབ་གསུམ་ཕྱག་དྲུག་(9b4)ཕྱག་དྲུག་ལ་གཡས་དང་པོ་ན་སྟོང་གི་འཇིག་ཊེན་འཁོར་ཡུག་ཏུ་བཙལ་པ།བར་མ་ན་རྡོ་རྗེ་སྣ་མ་ན་བན་ཊ་དམར་གིས་བཀང་(9b5)ད་གཡོན་དང་པོ་དང་ན་དག་སྐྱབར་མ་ན་རལ་གྲི་མཐ་མ་ན་ཡེ་ཤེས་ཀྱི་གཏོ་ལ་སྐལ་པའི་མྲེ་དཔུང་གི་དཀྱིལ་ན་སྨུལ་དང་(9b6)སྟོད་སྨྲེང་གིས་སྐུ་ལ་བརྒྱན་ཅིང་འཇིགས་ཆལ་རྣམ་པ་སྣ་ཚོགས་དང་སྟྲན་ཊེ།ཡུམ་གྲོ་ཏེ་ཤྲ་རེ་ཡང་བརྒྱན་དང་ཚ་ལུགས་(9b7)གཙོ་པོ་དང་མཐུན་བ་ལ་དྲུ་རྒྱན་སྦྲེད་པ་ཅིག་གཡོན་ཕྱོགས་སུ་འཁྲིལ་ཅིང་འཇིགས་ཆལ་རྣམ་པ་སྣ་ཚོགས་དང་སྟྲན་(10a1)༈།ཞིན་བཟླས་བཞིན།།

(21)ཨོཾ་རཏྣ་མ་ཏུ་གྲོ་ཕྲི་ཏེ་ར་ཀ་མ་ཏ་ཙན་ཊྲ་ས་ན་དུ་སྟྲན་ད་ཀ་ཏུ་ན་པ་ཙ་ཧཱུྃ་ཕཊ་ཨོཾ་སུ་ཊུ་རད་ན་གྲོ་ཏེ་ཤྲ་རེ་ཧཱུྃ་ཕཊ་ཅེས་བརྗོད་པས།(10a2)སྟྲོ་ཕྱོགས་སུ་འཁོར་ལོ་འི་རྩིབས་ལ་གཏོད་སྤྲིན་པོ་མོ་བསྐོལ་བའི་གདན་སྟེངས་སུམ་ཊེ་ཐལ་སྐྱ་དུ་རིངས་ཀྱི་སྦྱར་མོ་བསྒུས་པའི་གདན་སྟེངས་སུ་བཙོམ་ལྡན་(10a3)འདས་རིན་པོ་ཆེ་རད་ན་ཊེ་ཊུ་གཱ་སྨ་མདོག་སེར་ནག།།དཔ་གསུམ་ཕྱག་དྲུག་ལ་གཡས་ཀྱི་དང་པོ་ན་སྟོང་གི་འཇིག་ཊེན་འཁོར་ཡུག་ཏུ་བཙལ་པ།བར་མ་ན་རྡོ་རྗེ་(10a4)བར་མ་ན་བན་ད་དམར་གིས་བཀང་བགཡོན་དང་པོ་ན་དག་སྲ་ཊེ།བར་མ་ན་རལ་གྲི།མཐམ་མ་ན་ཡེ་ཤེས་ཀྱི་གཏོ་ལ་སྐལ་པ་སྨྲེ་དཔུང་ཀྱི་དཀྱིལ་(10a5)ན་སྨུལ་དང་སྟོད་འཕྲེང་གྱིས་སྐུ་ལ་བརྒྱན་ཅིང་ཡུམ་རད་ན་གྲོ་ཏེ་ཤྲ་རེ་དང་རྒྱན་དང་ཚ་ལུགས་གཙོ་པོ་དང་མཐུན་བ་གདབ་རྒྱན་སྦྲེད་པ་ཅིག།ཞིན་བསྐོལ་(10a6)བའི་གདན་སྟེངས་སུ་འཇིགས་ཆལ་སྣ་ཚོགས་དང་སྟྲན་ཊེ།།ག་ཉིས་སུ་སྦྲེད་པར་གཡོན་ཕྱོགས་སུ་འཁྲིལ་པར་བསམ་མོ།།

(22)ཨོཾ་པད་མ་ཕྲི་ཏེ་ར་ག་(10a7)མ་ཏ་ཚན་ད་ས་ན་དུ་སྟྲན་ད་ཀ་ཏུ་ན་པ་ཙ་ཧཱུྃ་ཕཊ་ཨོཾ་ཊེ་ཞ་ཏ་པ་ག་མཁ་མ་ཏུ་གྲོ་ཏེ་ཤྲ་རེ་ཕྱེ་ཤ་ཕྲི་ཤུད་ཊེ་ཧཱུྃ་ཕཊ་ཅེས་བརྗོད་པས།ནུབ་ཕྱོགས་སུ་འཁོར

ཨོ་(10b1)འི་རྩིབས་ལ་སྲིན་པོ་པོ་མོ་བསྒྱལ་པ་གཟིག་གི་སྤྲར་མོས་བསྒྲས་པའི་གདན་སྟེངས་སུ་བཙམ་ལྷན་འདས་པད་མ་ཕྲི་ཏི་ཏུ་ཀཱ་ཀྲ་མདོག་དམར་གནག(10b2)དབུ་གསུམ་ཕྱག་དྲུག་ལ་གཡས་དང་པོ་ན་སྟོང་གི་འཇིག་རྟེན་འཁོར་ཡུག་ཏུ་བཅས་པ་འབར་མ་རྡོ་རྗེ་མཐའ་མ་ན་བན་ད་དམར་གིས་བཀང་བ(10b3)གཡོན་དབུ་དབྱུ་སྟ་སྟེ་བར་མ་ན་རལ་གྲི་སྟེ་མཐའ་མ་ན་ཡེ་ཤེས་ཀྱི་གཏོལ་ཀྲ་ལྐ་པ་སྟེ་དབྱུང་གི་དཀྱིལ་ན་སྒྲལ་དང་ཕོད་འཕྱེང་གིས་ལུས་ལ་རྒྱན(10b4)ཅེད་ཕྱུམ་པད་མ་གྲོ་ཏི་ཤུ་རི་ཡང་རྒྱན་དང་ཚ་ལུགས་གཙོ་པོ་དང་མཐུན་པ་ལས་གདུ་རྒྱན་ཆྱེད་པ་ཅིག་ཞིང་བསྒྲལ་བའི་གདན་སྟེངས་སུ།(10b5)འཇིགས་ཆུལ་རྣམ་པ་སྣ་ཚོགས་ཀྱིས་བརྒྱན་ཏེ་གཡོན་ཕྱོགས་སུ་འབྱིལ་བར་བསམ་མོ།།

(23)ཨོཾ་ཀར་མ་མ་ད་ཕྲི་ཏི་ཏུ་ཀ་མ་ད་ཙན་ད་ས་ན་དུ་ཕྱུན་(10b6)ད་ཀ་ད་ན་པ་ཙ་ཏུ་པད། ཨོཾ་མ་ད་ཨ་མོ་ཀ་ཏུ་པད་ཆེས་བརྗོད་པས།བྱང་ཕྱོགས་སུ་འཕོར་ལོ་འི་རྩིབས་ལ་གགཱིན་རྗེ་པོ་མོ་བསྒྱལ་པའི་གདན་སྟེངས་(10b7)ལུག་གི་སྤྲར་མོས་བསྒྲས་པའི་སྟེངས་ན་ཁ་བཙམ་ལྷན་འདས་ཀར་མ་ཏི་ཏུ་ཀ་མ་ཀྲུ་མདོག་ལྗང་གནག་གདབ་གསུམ་ཕྱག་དྲུག་གཡས་ཀྱི་དང་པོ་ན་(10b8)སྟོང་གི་འཇིག་རྟེན་འཁོར་ཡུག་ཏུ་བཅས་པ་འབར་མ་ན་རྡོ་རྗེ་མཐའ་མ་ན་བན་ད་དམར་གིས་བཀང་བ།གཡོན་དབུ་སྒྲ་སྟབར་མ་ན་རལ་གྲི་མཐའ་མ་ན་བ་ན་ད་དམར་གིས(11a1)༡༽ཡེ་ཤེས་ཀྱི་གཏོལ།།ཀྲ་ལ་པ་ཁྱེ་དབྱུང་ཀྱི་དཀྱིལ་ན་སྒྲལ་དང་འཕོད་འཕྱེང་གིས་སྣ་ལ་བརྒྱན་ཏེ།།ཕྱུམ་ཀར་མ་གྲོ་ཏི་ཤུ་རི་ཡང་རྒྱན(11a2)དང་ཚ་ལུགས་དང་གཙོ་པོ་དང་མཐུན་གདབ་རྒྱན་ཆྱེད་པ་གཅིག་གཡོན་ཕྱོགས་སུ་འཕྱིལ་ཏེ།ཞིང་བསྒྱལ་བའི་གདན་སྟེངས་ན་འཇིགས་ཆུལ་སྣ་(11a3)ཚོགས་དང་གཉིས་སུ་ཆྱེད་པར་འཕྱིལ་བར་བསམ་མོ།།

(24)དེའི་ཕྱི་རིམ་ཕར་ཕྱོགས་ཀྱི་སྒོ་འབྱར་ཞིང་བརྒྱུང་པའི་གདན་སྟེངས་སུ་བ་ཇཱ་ཀིལུ་རི་ཏུ་ཞེས་(11a4)བརྗོད་པས་བཱ་ཇཱ་ཀིལུ་རི་ཏཱ་ཀྲུ་མདོག་སྔོན་མོ།ཞལ་གཅིག་ཕྱག་གཉིས།ཕྱག་གཡས་པ་ཞིང་དབྱུག་པ་འཕུར་བ།ཕྱུག་གཡོན་པ་བན་ད་(11a5)དམར་གིས་བཀང་བ་ཞལ་དུ་གསོལ་བར་བསམ་མོ།།སྒོ་ཕྱོགས་ཀྱི་སྒོ་འབྱུར་ལ་ཞིང་བརྒྱུང་བའི་གདན་སྟེངས་སུ་བ་ཇཱ་ཅེ་ཏུ་རི་ཏུ་ཞེས་བརྗོད་པས།བ་ཇཱ་ཅེ་ཏུ(11a6)རི་ཏཱ་ཀྲུ་མདོག་སེར་མོ།ཞལ་གཅིག་ཕྱག་གཉིས།ཕྱག་རྒྱ་མདའ་གཞུ་འགེངས་ཏེ་གཙོ་པོའི་ཐུགས་ཀར་བསྐུལ་བར་བསམ་མོ།།ཞུ་ཕྱོགས་ཀྱི་(1

1a7)སློ་འབུར་ལ་ཞིང་རྒྱུང་པའི་གདན་སྟེངས་སུ་བ་རྫ་པུ་མོ་ཏུ་ཞེས་བརྫོད་པས་ན་རྫ་པུ་མོ་
ཏུ་ཀླུ་མདོག་དམར་མོ་ཞལ་གཅིག་ཕྱག་གཉིས་ཕྱག་ན་རྒྱུ་ཤིན་གྱི་(11b1)རྒྱལ་མཚན་གྱི་རྒྱལ་
མཚན་བསྣམས་པ་། །བྱུང་ཕྱོགས་ཀྱི་སློ་འབུར་ཞིང་རྒྱུང་པའི་གདན་སྟེངས་སུ་བ་རྫ་པེ་ཏུ་ལི་རྒྱ་
མདོག་ནག་མོ་ཞལ་གཅིག་ཕྱག་(11b2)གཉིས་ཕྱག་གཡས་པ་རྫོ་རྗེ་དགུག་ཅིང་གསོལ་བ། །
ཕྱག་གཡོན་པ་ཞིང་གི་ཚེད་པ་བཟུང་སྟེ་ཞལ་དུ་གསོལ་བའི་དག་ཀུན་ཀྱང་ཞལ་གདངས་
སྤྲུ་(11b3)དགྲད་མཆེ་བ་བཚིགས་སྐྲལ་པའི་སྤྱི་དཔུང་གྱིས་འབར་བའི་དགྱིལ་ན་སྒྲུལ་དང་
ཐོད་འཕེང་གིས་སྐུ་ལ་བརྒྱན་པ་འཇིགས་ཚུལ་རྣམ་པ་སྔ་རྔོགས་(11b4)དང་ཕྱན་ཏེ་གཉིས་
སུ་བྱེད་པར་གཡོན་ཕྱོགས་སུ་འཁྱིལ་པར་བསམ་མོ། །དེའི་ཕྱི་རིས་ཤར་སྐྱོ་མཚམས་ཀྱི་གྲུ་ཆད་
ལ་ཞིང་རྒྱུང་པའི་གདན་སྟེངས་(11b5)བ་རྫ་པུ་ཀ་སི་ཞེས་བརྫོད་པས་ཁ་རྫ་པུ་ཀ་སི་སྐུ་
མདོག་དམར་སེར་ཞལ་གཅིག་ཕྱག་གཉིས་ཕྱག་གཡས་པས་ཞིང་གི་མགོ་བོ་ནས་མནན།
གཡོན་པས་(11b6)ཞིང་གི་ཙྭེད་པ་ནས་བཟུང་སྟེ་རྒྱུ་ཚོལ་དང་ནང་འགྲོལ་ཞལ་དུ་བསྟབས་
པར་བསམ་མོ། །སྦྱོ་ནུབ་མཚམས་ཀྱི་གྲུ་ཆད་ལ་ཞིང་རྒྱུང་པའི་གདན་(11b7)སྟེངས་སུ་བ་རྫ་
གས་ཨ་རི་ཞེས་བརྫོད་པས་གས་ཨ་རི་སྐུ་མདོག་ལྗང་ཁ་ཞལ་གཅིག་ཕྱག་གཉིས་ཕྱག་གཡོན་
པས་བན་དུ་དམར་གིས་བཀང་བ་(11b8)ཕྱག་གཡས་པས་རྫོ་རྗེ་ཙེ་དགུས་ཞལ་དུ་གསོལ། །
ཐུབ་བྱུང་མཚམས་ཀྱི་གྲུ་ཆད་ཞིང་རྒྱུང་པའི་གདན་སྟེངས་སུབ་རྫ་སྣ་ན་ནི(12a1)༈ཞེས་
བརྫོད་པས་ན་རྫ་སྣ་ན་ནི་སྐུ་མདོག་མཐིང་ཀ་ཞལ་གཅིག་ཕྱག་གཉིས་གཡས་པ་ཞིང་གྱི་ཀུང་
པ་བཟུང་།གཡོན་པས་མགོ་ཙོ་ནས་བཟུང་སྟེ་ཅི་ཏུ་ཚེམས་(12a2)གིས་འདེན་པར་བསམ་
མོ། །བྱང་ཤར་མཚམས་ཀྱི་གྲུ་ཆད་ལ་ཞིན་བརྒྱུང་བའི་གདན་སྟེངས་སྐུབ་རྫ་ཙན་ད་ལི་སྐུ་
མདོག་གསེར་སྐྱ་ཞལ་གཅིག་ཕྱག་གཉིས།(12a3)ཕྱག་གཡོན་པ་ཞིང་གྱི་ཀེད་པ་བཟུང་།
གཡས་པ་བན་ད་དང་གྱིས་བཅད་དེ།གཙོ་བོ་ལ་བསྟབས་པར་བསམ་མོ། །དེ་དག་ཀུན་ཀྱང་
སྐལ་པའི་སྤྱི་དཔུང་འབར་(12a4)བའི་དགྱིལ་ན་སྒྲུལ་དང་ཐོད་འཕེང་གྱིས་སྐུ་ལ་བརྒྱན་
ཅིང་།ཞལ་གདངས་སྤྲུན་དགྲད་མཆེ་བ་བཚིགས་ཏེ་ཁྲོ་ཚུལ་རྣམ་པ་སྔ་ཚོགས་དང་ཕྲན་སྟེ་
གཉིས་(12a5)སུ་བྱེད་པར་གཡོན་ཕྱོགས་སུ་འཁྱིལ་བར་བསམ་མོ། །

(25)དེའི་ཕྱི་རིམ་ཤར་ཕྱོགས་སུ་འབར་བའི་བར་ཁྱམས་ཞིང་རྒྱང་པའི་གདན་སྟེང་སུ།(12a6) བསྐལ་དེ་བཞུགས་པར་བསམ་མོ།།སྟོ་ཕྱོགས་ཀྱི་འབར་བའི་བར་ཁྱམས་ཞིང་རྒྱང་པའི་གདན་ སྟེངས་སུབ་ཧྲྃ་ཀྲི་ཤུ་ཁ་དེ་(12a7)ཞེས་བཏོད་པས་ཁབ་ཛྲ་ཧཱུ་ཀྲི་ཤུ་ཁ་སྐུ་མདོག་དམར་མོ་ཡལ་ །ཕྱག་ཀྱི་མགོ་ཅན་ཕྱག་རྒྱ་རྒྱ་གྲགས་དཔུང་མགོར་བསྐྱལ་པ།(12b1)ཅེ་ད་ཚེམས་ཀྱིས་དངས་ ནས་ཞིང་ལ་འགྲོ་ཆྱགས་སུ་གཟིགས་པར་བསམ་མོ།།ཤུབ་ཕྱོགས་སུ་འབར་བའི་བར་ཁྱམས་(1 2b2)ཞིང་རྒྱང་པའི་གདན་སྟེངས་སུ་ཁབ་ཛྲ་སྟི་ལ་སྐུ་ཁ་དེ་ཞེས་བཏོད་པས་ཁབ་ཛྲ་སྟི་ལ་སྐུ་ཁ་ སྐུ་མདོག་གནག་མོ་ལྱ་འི་མགོ་ཅན་(12b3)ཕྱག་གཉིས་ཀྱིས་ཞིང་ཀྱི་ཤུན་བརྒྱས་སྟེ་གཡང་ བའི་ལ་འཛིན་པར་བསམ་མོ།།བྱང་ཕྱོགས་ཀྱི་འབར་བའི་བར་ཁྱམས་ཞིང་རྒྱང་པའི་(12b4) གདན་སྟེངས་སུབ་ཛྲ་ཤུ་ན་སྐུ་ཁ་དེ་ཞེས་བཏོད་པས་ཁབ་ཛྲ་ཤུ་ན་སྐུ་མདོག་མཐིང་གནག་ །སྐྱུང་མོའི་མགོ་ཅན་འཁས་གཡས་པས་(12b5)ཞིང་ཀྱི་མགོ་ནས་བརྗེས་པ་གཡོན་པས་ཀྲང་ པས་ཀྲང་པ་ནས་བརྗེས་པ་ཕྱག་གཉིས་ཀྱིས་རྒྱ་ཚིལ་དངའང་གྲོལ་ཞལ་དུ་(12b6)གསོལ་བ།། ཤར་སྟོ་ཚམས་ཀྱི་འབར་བའི་བར་ཁྱམས་ཞིང་རྒྱང་པའི་གདན་སྟེངས་སུ་བ་ཛྲ་ཀྱི་ཏ་སྐུ་ཁ་སྐུ་ མདོག་དམར་མོ་(12b7)བྱ་ཁྱོད་ཀྱི་མགོ་ཅན་ཕྱག་གཡས་པས་ཟྲ་ཛྲ་དངས་ཀྱིས་བཀང་བ། ཕྱག་གཡོན་པས་རང་འགྲི་སྐྲམས་པ།།སྟོ་ནུབ་ཚམས།(13a1)༢༠།།ཀྱི་འབར་བའི་བར་ཁྱམས་ ཞིང་རྒྱང་པའི་གདན་སྟེངས་ནུབ་ཛྲ་ཀང་ཀ་སྐུ་ཁ་སྐུ་མདོག་སེར་མོ་ཉུར་བྱའི་མགོ་ཅན།།(13 a2)ཕྱག་གཡས་གཉིས་ཀྱིས་ཞིང་ཀྱི་ཤུན་བརྒྱས་སྟེ་ཀྲང་པ་རེ་རེ་བཀལ་ཏེ་ཕྱག་པ་ལ་བསྐལ་ བའཤུབ་བྱང་ཚམས་ཀྱི་འབར་བའི་བར་(13a3)ཁྱམས་ཞིང་རྒྱང་པའི་གདན་སྟེངས་ནབ་ ཛྲ་ཁ་ཁ་སྐུ་ག་དེ་ཞེས་བཏོད་པས།ཁ་ཁ་སྐུ་མདོག་གནག་མོ་བྱ་རོག(13a4)ཀྱི་མགོ་ཅན། ཕྱག་གཡས་པ་ཟྲ་འཛུ་དམར་ཀྱིས་བཀང་ག་ཕྱག་གཡོན་པས་ཀང་འགྲི་བསྩམས་པ།བྱང་ཤར་ ཚམས་ཀྱི་འབར་(13a5)བའི་བར་ཁྱམས་ཞིང་རྒྱང་པའི་གདན་སྟེངས་ནབ་ཛྲ་ཏུ་ལྱ་སྐུ་ཁ་དེ་ ཞེས་བཏོད་པས།ཏུ་ལྱ་སྐུ་ཁ་སྐུ་མདོག་དུད་ཀ་ཨུག་པའི་མགོ་ཅན(13a6)ཕྱག་གཡས་པ་ཟྲ་ཛྲ་ དམར་ཀྱིས་བཀང་ག་གཡོན་པ་རོ་རྗེ་ཚུགས་ཀྱིས་འགུགས་པའི་དག་ཀུན་ཀྱང་སྐྲལ་པའི་ཁྱེ་

དཔུང་འབར་(13a7)བའི་དཀྱིལ་ན།།སྤྱལ་དང་ཕོད་ཁེང་ཀྱིས་སྐུ་ལ་བརྒྱན་པ།།ཞལ་གདངས་
སྟུན་དགྱད་མཆེ་བ་གཙིགས་པ་འ།(13b1)འཇིགས་ཆུལ་ནྀ་པ་སྟུ་ཚོགས་དང་ལྷན་ནེ་བཞུགས་
པར་བསམ་མོ།།

(26)དེའི་ཕྱི་རིམ་ཞར་ཕྱོགས་ཀྱི་སྒོ་ཁྱུད་ལ་ཞིང་ཀྱུང་པའི་(13b2)གདན་སྟེངས་ན།ཁ་ཌྟ་ཨ་
ཏུ་ཏིང་ཅེ་ཏུ་ཡང་ཞེས་བརྗོད་པས།ཏུ་གདོང་ལྷགས་ཀྱུ་མ་སྨྲ་མདོག་དཀར་མོ།ཕྱག་གཡས་ན་
ལྷགས་ཀྱུ་སྣམས་(13b3)ཕྱག་གཡོན་ན་ཞང་འགྲི་སྣམས་པ།སྤྱལ་དང་ཕོད་ཁེང་ཀྱིས་སྐུ་ལ་
བརྒྱན་བ།།ཞལ་སྔོར་གཟིགས་ཤིང་ཁྲོ་ཆུལ་ཏུ་བཞུགས་(13b4)པར་བསམ་མོ།།ལྷོ་ཕྱོགས་ཀྱི་
སྒོ་ཁྱུད་ཞིང་ཀྱུང་པའི་གདན་སྟེངས་ནཁ་ཌྟ་ཨ་མོ་གཱ་ཏུང་ཞེས་བརྗོད་པས་ཐཔ་གདོང་
ཞགས་(13b5)པ་མ་སྨྲ་མདོག་སྤོན་མོ།ཕྱག་གཡས་པ་ན་ཞགས་པ།གཡོན་ཐཔ་རོན་ཀྱི་མཆེ་བ་
གཙིགས་སྟེ།ཁྲོ་ཆུལ་དུ་བཞུགས་པར་བསམོ།(13b5)ནུབ་ཕྱོགས་ཀྱི་སྒོ་ཁྱུད་ཞིང་ཀྱུང་པའི་
གདན་སྟེངས་ནཁ་ཌྟ་ལོ་ཀ་བམ་ཞེས་བརྗོད་པས།ཌྟ་ཌྩེ་ཉི་ཟླ་སྤྲུན་སྐུ་མདོག་དམར་མོ་ཞལ་
ཅིག་(13b7)ཕྱག་གཉིས།ཕྱག་གཡས་ན་ཌྟ་ཌྩེ།གཡོན་ལྷགས་ཀྱུ་སྣམས་པ།ཞལ་སྔོར་གཟིགས་
ཞིང་སྤྱལ་དང་ཕོད་ཁེང་ཀྱིས་སྐུ་ལ་(14a1)༠།།བརྒྱན་ཏེ་བཞུགས་པར་བསམ་མོ།།བྱང་ཕྱོགས་
ཀྱི་སྒོ་ཁྱུད་ཞིང་ཀྱུང་བའི་གདན་སྟེངས་ནཁ་ཌྟ་པ་སྨྲི་བ་ལ་དེ་ཏོ་ཞེས་བརྗོད་(14a2)པས།
ཐལ་བྱེད་ཌྟལ་བྱས་མ་སྨྲ་མདོག་ལྗང་གུ་ཞལ་གཅིག།ཕྱག་གཉིས།ཕྱག་གཡས་པ་ན་ཌྟ་ཌྩེ།ཌྟལ་
བུ།གཡོན་པ་ན་སྟུན་འཐ་དམར་གིས་(14a3)བཀང་བ།ཀྲུམ་ཅིག་ཏུ་གཡོན་བན་འདབ་
དམར་གིས་བཀང་བའི་བསྟེ་དུ།ཌྟ་རྒྱ་གྲགས་ཀྱིས་ཁ་བཏད་དེ།དེའི་སྟེང་དུ་དཔལ་སྦུང་བ་
མཐབ་(14a4)ཡས་སྨྲ་མདོག་ལེབ་བརྒྱ་མཚོན་གང་བའི་ཕྱག་ན་ཌྟ་བུ་སྣམས་པ་པ་ཞེས་
ཀྱུང་འབྱུག་དེ་དག་ཀུན་ཀྱུང་སྐལ་པའི་མྱེ་དཔུང་གི་དཀྱིལ་ན།།(14a5)འཇིགས་ཐྱེད་ཆེན་པོ་
འི་ཆ་ལུགས་སྨྲ་འཚོགས་དང་སྟུན་ཏེ་བཞུགས་པར་བསམ་མོ།།

(27)དེའི་ཕྱི་རིམ་ཞར་ཕྱོགས་གི་འབར་བའི་བར་ཁྱམས་ཞིང་རས་མའི་གདན་(14a6)སྟེངས་
ན།།ཌྟུཾ་ཌྲུ་ཌྲུ་ཌྲུ་ཌྲུ་ཀྲུ།།ཞེས་བརྗོད་པས།།ཧར་དང་པོ་ན་ཌྟི་ཝི་ཞིན་མོ་མདོག་ན།།ཁྱུག་གཡས་
སྣན་འདའ་དམར་ཀྱིས་བཀང་བ།།གཡོན་ཌྟོ་ཌྩེ་སྣམས་པ།(14a7)ཞར་གཉིས་པ་ན་འཚོངས་

མ་སྐུ་མངོག་དཀར་མོ།།གངོང་བཞི་རྭ་ཕྱུག་གཡས་པ་ན་པད་མ་དཀར་པོ་སྐྱམས་ད།།གཡོན་ངོ་
ཊེ་སྐྱམས་པ།།ཕར་གསུམ་(14a8)པ་ན་ཁྲོ་མོ་སྐུ་མངོག་དམར་སེར།།ཕྱུག་གཡས་ན་ཊི་ཤུ་ལ།།
གཡོན་པ་ངོ་ཊེ་ཊེ་སྐྱམས་པ།།ཕར་བཞི་པར་ན་དབང་མོ་སྐུ་མངོག་དཀར་མོ།།(14b1)ཕྱུག་
གཡས་པ་ན་ཨིན་དུ་བ་ཊོ།།གཡོན་ངོ་ཊེ་ཊེ།།ཕར་ལྔ་པ་ན་འཇུག་སྲེ་དཀྲུ་མངོག་སྟོན་མོ།།ཕྱུག་
གཡས་ན་འགོར་ལོ།།གཡོན་ངོ་ཊེ་ཊེ།།ཕར་དྲུག་པ་(14b2)ན་གཟི་ནུ་སྐུ་མངོག་དམར་ཕྱུག་
གཡས་ན་མདུང་གཡོན་ངོ་ཊེ་ཊེ།།དེ་དག་ཀུན་ཀྱང་ཞིང་རས་མའི་གཅན་སྟེངས་ག།།རང་གི་ལག་
ཆ་དང་ཆས་ནས་ཆེ་(14b3)བགྱི་ཞེས་ཆས་ཏེ།།འཕོད་པར་བསམ་མོ།།སྟོ་ཕྱོགས་ཀྱི་འབར་བའི་
བར་ཁྱམས་ལ།།སྟུ་སྟུ་སྟུ་སྟུ་སྟུ་ཞེས་བརྗོད་པས།།སྟོ་དང་པོ་ན་ཞི་བ་མོ་སྐུ་མངོག་དཀར་མོ།
(14b4)ཕྱུག་གཡས་པ་ན་པད་མ་དཀར་མོ་བསྣམས་པ།།གཡོན་ངོ་ཊེ་ཊེ་སྐྱམས་པ།།སྟོ་གཉིས་པ་ན་
བདུད་ཊི་མོ་སྐུ་མངོག་དམར་མོ།།ཕྱུག་གཡས་པད་མ་དམར་པོ་(14b5)སྐྱམས་པ།།གཡོན་ངོ་ཊེ་
ཊེ།།སྟོ་གསུམ་པ་ན་ངོ་ཊེ་ཊེ་དམར་མོ་སྐུ་མངོག་དམར་སེར།།ཕྱུག་གཡས་པད་མ་དཀར་མོ།།
གཡོན་ངོ་ཊེ་ཊེ་ཞི་ཁྲོ་སྟོམས་(14b6)པའི་འཆུལ་དུ་བཞུགས།།པར་བསམ་མོལ་[lacuna]
(14b7)།སྟོ་ལྷ་པ་ན་ཞིན་མོ་སྨེ་སྦྲེང་སྐུ་མངོག་(14b8)ནག་མོ།།ཕྱུག་གཡས་པ་ན་ཊྲན་འདའ།
གཡོན་ངོ་ཊེ་ཊེ་ཞི་ཁྲོ་སྟོམས་པའི་འཆུལ་དུ་བཞུགས་པར་བསམ་མོ།།སྟོ་དྲུག་པ་ན་ཟབ་ན་མོ་སྐུ་
མངོག་དམར་(15a1) ༢།སེར་ཕྱུག་གཡས་པ་ན་ཞིང་གི་ཀྱུ་ཞགས་འཛིན།།ཕྱུག་གཡོན་ངོ་ཊེ་
སྐྱམས་ག།།དེ་དག་ཀུན་ཀྱང་ཞིང་རས་མ་འི་གཅན་སྟེངས་ན།།རང་གི་(15a2)ལག་ཆ་དང་
ཆས་ཏེ་འཕོད་པར་བསམ་མོ།།ཉུབ་ཕྱོགས་གི་འབར་བའི་ཁྱམས་ཞིང་རས་མ་འི་གཅན་སྟེངས་
སུ་ཏྲུ་ཏྲུ་ཏྲུ་ཏྲུ་ཏྲུ་ཞེས་བརྗོད་པས།(15a3)ནུབ་དང་པོ་ན་དག་པ་མོ་སྐུ་མངོག་དམར་མོ།།
ཕྱུག་གཡས་པ་ན་ཟབ་འགྲོ།།གཡོན་ངོ་ཊེ་ཞི་ཁྲོ་ཆུལ་དུ་བཞུགས་པར་བསམ་མོ།།ཉུབ་གཉིས་པ་
ན་ཡིད་(15a4)འཕྲོག་མ་སྐུ་མངོག་དམར་མོ།།ཕྱུག་གཡས་པ་ན་འདའ་ལུ།།གཡོན་ངོ་ཊེ་སྐྱམས་
ཞི་ཁྲོ་ཆུལ་དུ་བཞུགས་པར་བསམ་མོ།།ཉུབ་གསུམ་ན་སྒྲུབ་མོ་(15a5)སྐུ་མངོག་དཀར་མོ།།
ལྦའི་མགོ་ཅན་ཕྱུག་གཡས་པ་ན་འཆོམ་འབུ་ཊོ་ཊེ།ཅན།།གཡོན་པ་ངོ་ཊེ་ཊེ་ཞི་ཁྲོ་སྟོམས་པ་འི་
ཆུལ་དུ་བཞུགས་པར་བསམ་མོ།།(15a6)ཉུབ་བཞི་པའ་ན་གཏིག་བུ་སྦྲོང་མ་སྐུ་མངོག་དམར་
སེར།།ཕྱུག་གཡས་པ་ན་ཀ་ཊ་རེ།།གཡོན་པ་ངོ་ཊེ་ཊེ་ཞི་ཁྲོ་འི་ཆུལ་དུ་བཞུགས་པར་བསམ་མོ།།(15

b1)ཉུབ་དྲུག་པ་ན་གསོད་བྱེད་མ་སྐུ་མདོག་དམར་མོ་ཕྱག་གཡས་པ་རལ་གྲི་གཡོན་རོ་རྗེ་ཞི་
ཁྲོ་སྟོངས་པའི་ཚུལ་དུ་བཞུགས་པར་བསམ་མོ་།།བྱུང་ཕྱོགས་(15b2)གི་འབར་བའི་པར་ཁྲམས་
ཞིང་རས་མ་འི་གདན་སྟེངས་སུ་།།ཕྱྭོ་ཕྱྭི་ཕྱྭུ་ཕྱྭེ་ཕྱྭོ་ཞིས་བརྗོད་པས་བྱུང་དྲུང་(sic)པོ་ན་རླུང་
མོ་སྐུ་མདོག་ནག་མོ་ཕྱག་གཡས་(15b3)པ་ན་རྣན་འདའ་གཡོན་རོ་རྗེ་ཞི་ཁྲོ་ཚུལ་དུ་
བཞུགས་པར་བསམ་མོ།།བྱུང་གཉིས་པ་ན་ཀྱི་མོ་སྐུ་མདོག་དམར་སེར་ཕྱག་གཡས་པ་ན་(15b
4)གསལ་ཞེད་གཡོན་རོ་རྗེ་ཞི་ཁྲོའི་ཚུལ་དུ་བཞུགས་པར་བསམ་མོ།།བྱུང་ཕྱོགས་ས་(sic)པ་ན་
འཕག་མོ་སྐུ་མདོག་དམར་ནག་ཕྱག་གཡས་(15b5)མཆེ་བ་གཡོན་རོ་རྗེ་ཞི་ཁྲོའི་ཚུལ་དུ་
བཞུགས་པར་བསམ་མོ།།བྱུང་བཞི་པ་ན་དཀྲ་བྱུང་མོ་སྐུ་མདོག་དམར་སྨུག་ཕྱག་གཡས་བྱེས་
རྒྱུ་(15b6)གཙིན་པོ་ལ་བསྟོབས་པ་ཕྱག་གཡོན་རོ་རྗེ་ཞི་ཁྲོའི་ཚུལ་དུ་བཞུགས་པར་བསམ་མོ།།
(16a1)༡།།བྱུང་དྲུག་པ་ན་ཚུའི་ལྷ་མོ་སྐུ་མདོག་དཀར་མོ་།།ཀྱུ་སྲིན་གི་མགོ་ཅན་ཕྱག་གཡས་
སྦྱལ་འཕགས་གཡོན་རོ་རྗེ་ཞི་ཁྲོའི་ཚུལ་དུ་བཞུགས་པར་(16a2)བསམ་མོ།།དེ་དག་ཀུན་ཀྱང་ཞིང་
རས་མ་འི་གདན་སྟེངས་ན་རང་གི་ལག་ཅ་དང་ཚམ་ཏེ་ཅི་བགྱི་ཅི་བགྱི་ཞིས་ཆས་ཏེ་འབོད་
པར་བསམ་མོ།།དེ་འི་སྐྱོ་(16a3)བཟིར་ཞིང་རས་མ་འི་གདན་སྟེངས་སུ་ཕྱྭོ་ཕྱྭུ་ཕྱྭོ་ཞིས་
བརྗོད་པས་ཤར་ཕྱོགས་ཀི་སྒོ་བྱུད་ལ་ནག་མོ་ཆེན་མོ་སྐུ་མདོག་ནག་མོ་ཕྱག་གཡས་(16a4)པ་
ལྕགས་ཀྱུ་གཡོན་རོ་རྗེ་ཁྲོའི་ཚུལ་དུ་བཞུགས་པར་བསམ་མོ།།ལྷོ་ཕྱོགས་ཀི་སྒོ་བྱུད་ལ་ར་མགོ་ན་
སྐུ་མདོག་དམར་སེར་ཕྱག་གཡས་ན་(16a5)ཞགས་པ་གཡོན་རོ་རྗེ་ཁྲོའི་ཚུལ་དུ་བཞུགས་པར་
བསམ་མོ།།ནུབ་ཕྱོགས་ཀི་སྒོ་བྱུད་ལ་འཕྲམ་ནུ་མ་སྐུ་མདོག་ཕྱོན་ག་མོ་ཕྱག་གཡས་(16a6)
ལྕགས་བསྒྲོགས་གཡོན་པའ་རོ་རྗེ་ཁྲོའི་ཚུལ་དུ་བཞུགས་པར་བསམ་མོ།།བྱུང་ཕྱོགས་ཀི་སྒོ་བྱུད་ལ་
གསུམ་འཛིན་གི་ཚུན་མ།།སྐུ་མདོག་(16a7)ནག་མོ་ཕྱག་གཡས་དྲིལ་བུ་གཡོན་པ་རོ་རྗེ་།།དེ་
དག་ཀུན་ཀྱང་བསྐལ་པ་འི་མྱེ་དཔུང་གི་དཀྱིལ་ན་ཞིང་རས་མའི་གདན་སྟེངས་ན་རང་གི་(16
b1)ལག་ཅ་དང་ཆས་ཏེ་ཅི་བགྱི་ཅི་བགྱི་ཞིས་ཆས་ཏེ་འབོད་པར་བསམ་མོ།
(28)དེ་ཡང་ཅི་མཛོ་ཞིས་ག།ཤྲྱུད་དེ་ཉིད་ལས་འདི་སྐད་ཅེས་བརྗོད་པར་བྱ་ག།ས་ལས་(1
6b2)བཀྲགས་པ་ཕྱག་རྒྱར་བྱ།།ནམ་འགྲོལ་རིས་པར་ཐོབ་འགྱུར་ནས་དག་པའི་ཡེ་ཞེས་
སྦྱངས་པ་ལས།སྐྱོམ་ཅི་དགོས་སྟེ་དེ་ཉིད་ཡིག།ཕྱོགས་འདུས་(16b3)དཀྱིལ་འབོར་བདག་

ཞིང་ཆེ༎ཀྱི་དཀྱིགས་ཐུགས་གི་དཀྱིལ་འཁོར་ནས༎དཀྱིལ་འཁོར་ཐམས་ཅད་སྤྲུན་དུང་དྷོ༎ཨོཾ་
ཟུ་ལུ་ཟུ་ལུ་ཧུང་ཕྱོ་བ་རྫ་(16b4)ས་མ་ཡ་ཧོཿ༎བ་རྫ་ས་མ་ཡ་སྐྱག་ན་རྫ་ས་མ་ཡ་ཧོཿ༎ཧཱུ་(s
ic)ནི་གྲུབ་པའི་སྐུ་འདི་རྣང་པོཿཧུང་ཁྲོ་ལ་ཁྲོས་པས་ནི་མཛད་པ་ཐུགས་རྗེ་ཁྲོས་(16b5)པས་
ཆམ་བ་འི་འཚོགས་འབར་བའི་བྲེ་རྣངས་དཀྲད་པོ་ཆེ་དེ་ཞིང་དུ་ནི་མཉམ་བསྟོར་བ་ཕྱུག༎
རྒྱལ་ཆེན་པོ་བདག་ལ་སྲུལ་ཨོཾ་ས་ས་(16b6)ཡ་ཨཱཿབ་རྫ་ས་མ་ཡ་ཕཊ་རམ་ཤ་ལི་ཤུ་ལི་ཏ་ལི་
ཏ་པ་ཏོ་ཀཧཿམ་གོ་ན་ཟུ་ཏེ་ཁ་རམ་ཡོ་གི་ནི་ཧུང་དུ་ཏེ་ཕཊ༎
(29)དེ་ལྟར་དཀྱིལ་འཁོར་(16b7)གསལ་བར་བགོད་ནས༎འཇིག་ཏེན་དྲུག་གི་ཕྱོགས་བཅུ་
དགའ༎མཐའ་དབུས་ཆྱེད་པར་ཁྱབ་པའི་དཀར་བའི་དཀྱིལ་འཁོར་གསལ་བར་སྐྱེད་(17a1)
༎༎སྨུག་གནས་མེར་ནས་ཕྱོ་གནས་དགའ་དམར་ནས་ལྗང་གནས་འཇིགས་པའི་སྐྱ་དངུ་
གསུམ་ཕྱུག་དྲུག་ཞབས་(17a2)བཞིར་དགྲག་ཕོད་ཆོན་གོས་ནི་སྣ་ཆོགས་ཀྱིག༎ཆམས་པའི་སྐུ་
ཆེན་འབྲུག་སྒྲོགས་པ༎སྐྲ་དང་ཕོད་ཆོན་གའི་བྲར་བཅས༎(17a3)སྟོང་གི་འཇིག་ཏེན་
འཁོར་ཁུག་ལྟར་རྫ་རྗེ་དུང་ཆེན་གང་བ་དངལ་གི་(sic)དུ་ལྟ་གཏོལ་ལས་བསྐོགས༎
རང་གི་ལག་ཅ་སྟ་(17a4)འཚོགས་དགའ་བཙུན་མོ་འཇིན་པའི་འཚོགས་དང་འཕྲེལ༎གནས་
དང་ཡུལ་གི་ཕྱག་རྒྱན་དགའི་ཐྱོ་མི་ཕྱུག་རྒྱན་རབ་མཛེས་ཤེ་དགླས་(17a5)དང་བྲན་མོ་ཁྲི་
མའི་འཚོགས་བཅུ་གཉིས་དང་ནི་བཀྱད་ཀྱིས་མཛེས་རང་གི་སྤྲུ་དང་ལགག་ཆར་བཅས༎ཨི་
བགྱི་ཞེས་ནི་ཆས་ཏེ་མངགས་ཆེས་བཏོད་པས༎(17a6)འཕྲོགས་བཅུ་ཐམས་ཅད་འབར་བའི་
དཀྱིལ་འཁོར་གསལ་བྲར་བགོད་ནས༎དེ་ལ་འདི་སྐད་ཆེས་བཏོད་པར་བྱའོ༎ཡན་ལག་མ་
ཅུམས་ཡོ་བྱད་(17a7)སྤྲ༎ཆོཿག་རྟོགས་པར་ཤེས་པ༎རྣལ་འབྱོར་འཚོགས་པའི་དཀྱིལ་
འཁོར་ཞིག༎རྟོགས་གྲུབ་ལས་རྣམས་རྟོགས་པར་ཐྱེག༎ནི་གྲུབ་(17b1)པའི་སྐུ་འདི་རྣང་བར་
བྱོ༎ཧཱུཾ་གཏུམ་ཆེན་དུས་མཉ་ཁྲི་སྤྲར་འབར་འོད་ཟེར་ནི་མ་འབྱམ་གི་གཟིབ་འཁྲིག་གཉེར་སྐྲིག
སྟོང་འགྱུར་བ་བཞིན༎(17b2)མཆེ་ད་ཟང་ཡག་ཟ་ཐྱེད་ཆེ་ཧོ་ཧྱུ་ཆམ་བའི་ང་རོ་འབྱུག་སྟོང་
འདིར་སྐྱུག་ཆེན་རི་རབ་འབྱུམ་རྗེལ་སྐྲགཨཿཨ་ལི་གང་རྒྱངས་ཆན་དྲུ་སྤྲུགས༎(17b3)པའི་
ཕོད་རྣང་གཡེམས་པ་ཆེ་ཧོཿཧུང་ཁྲོས་པའི་རྒྱལ་པོ་འོད་པོ་ཆེ་ཨི་ཤེས་དཀྱིལ་འཁོར་ཀུན་དུ་
གསལ་འབྲར་བའི་ཡེ་ཤེས་ཀུན་དུ་འཚོམས༎(17b4)སྟ་འཚོགས་ཡེ་ཤེས་ཐིག་ལེ་ཆེ་ཧོ༎ཧུང་

ཁྲོམས་པའི་རྒྱལ་པོ་སྟྱིན་ཆེན་པོ་འཕྲོས་ཏེ་དཀྱིལ་འཁོར་ཆར་བཞིན་འབེབས་དཀྱིལ་འཁོར་(17
b5)ཡིད་བཞིན་འབྱུང་པའི་གཏེར་ལྟ་འཚོགས་འཕྲོས་པས་ཐིག་ལེ་ཆེ་སྡོ་ཆུང་བདུད་ཀུན་གྱི་
ནི་བདག་ཆེན་པོ།བདུད་ཀྱི་བདུད་སྟེ་རྣམ་པར་(17b6)འཛོམས་འཛིགས་པའི་ཚོགས་ཡང་
འཛིགས་ཁྲེད་པའཛིགས་ཁྲེད་ཆེན་པོའི་ཐིག་ལེ་ཆེ་སྡོ།ཚི་དོ་རྗེ་ཐྲག་ཆེན་ས་བ་པོ་རྟོ་རྗེ་ཆུ་འོ་
སྱུད་(17b7)ཆེན་པོརྟོ་རྗེ་ཁྱི་སྟེ་ཀུན་འབར་ཆེ།རྟོ་རྗེ་ཐོང་ཁྱུང་གཡེངས་པ་ཆེ་སྡོ།
(30)དུ་ནི་འབར་བྲ་ཆེན་འཕོ་འི་དཀྱིལ་འཁོར་ཁདག་ཀྱི་ཕྱུང་པོ་དང་(17b8)འབབས་དང།
སྐྱེ་མཆེད་ལ་བསྟ་བར་བྱ་སྟེ།དེ་ལ་རྒྱུན་གི་ཏིང་ངེ་འཛིན་བསྒོམས་པའི་ཚོགས་བཀད་འདི་སྐད་
ཅེས་བརྗོད་པར་བྱའོ།།(18a1)ༀ།ཕྱུང་པོ་ལྷ་ལྷ་ཉིད་འཁྲུ་རྒྱལ་འཚོགས་ཆེན་པོ་རིགས་ཀྱི་དེ་
བཞིན་ཡུམ་སྐྱེ་མཆེད་ཁྲམས་རྣམས་ཅང་པོ་ཀུན།ཕྱུགས་རྗེ་ཅཙ་(18a2)བའི་དཀྱིལ་འཁོར་
འཚོགས་རྒྱུ་གཅིག་པ་དང་ཡིག་འབྱུ་འི་ཚུལ་ཁྲིན་ཀྱིས་རྣབས་དང་མཚོན་གསུ་པ་འབར་བ་དུ་
ཏོགས་པ་རྣམ་(18a3)བཞི་འིས་ཐབས་ཅང་མཚོན་རྟོགས་རྒྱལ་པོ་ཆེད་ནི་དཀྱིལ་འཁོར་
བསྒྲ་བྲར་བྱ་སྟེ།འབར་བའི་དཀྱིལ་འཁོར་བདག་ཀྱི་ཕྱུང་པོ་དང་ཁམས་(18a4)དང་སྐྱེ་མཆེད་
ལ་འདུས་ལ་ཕྱུང་པོ་དང་འཁམས་དང་སྐྱེ་མཆེད་ཡི་གི་ༀ་ལ་འདུས།ཡི་གི་ཏུང་ནི་ཡེ་ཤེས་ལྷ་
འི་ངོ་བོ་རྒྱལ་བ་རིགས་(18a5)ལྔ་འི་རང་བཞིན་ཏེ།དུ་ནི་བཙོམ་ལྡན་འདས་རྣམ་པར་སྣང་
མཛད་དེ་རིན་ཆེན་འབྱུང་ལྡན་ནི་སྣང་བ་མཐའ་ཡས་འཁབས(18a6)སྐྱེད་ནི་དོན་ཡོན་
གྲུབ་པའི་རང་བཞིན།ཐིག་ལེ་ནི་དོ་རྗེ་སེམས་པའརྒྱམ་གཅིག་ཏུ་དུ་ནི་ཚོས་ཀྱི་དབྱིངས་རྣམ་
པར་དག་པའི་(18a7)ཡི་ཤེསང་ནི་མཐམ་པ་ཉིད་ཀྱི་ཡི་ཤེས་ཁབས་བསྐྱེད་ནི་བྱ་བའ་ནན་
ཏན་བསྐྱབ་པའི་ཡི་ཤེསང་ནི་སོ་སོ་ཀུན་དུ་ཏོག་པའི་ཡི་ཤེས(18b1)ཐིག་ལེ་ནི་ཁྱི་ཁྲི་ལོང་ལྷ་
པུ་འི་ཡི་ཤེས།།ཡངརྣམ་གཅིག་དུ་སྐུ་དང་གསུང་དང་ཐུགས་ཀྱི་ཡང་བདག་ཉིད་དོ།།ཉི་སྐུ་
ནི་རང་བཞིན(18b2)ཞབས་སྐྱེད་ནི་གསུང་གི་རང་བཞིན།།ཐིག་ལེ་ནི་ཐུགས་ཀྱི་རང་བཞིན།
དེ་ལྟར་གསལ་བ་དྲིག་ཞབས་སྐྱེད་འ་ལ་ཐིགན་དུ་ལ་(18b3)ཐིགན་ཏུ་ང་ཟླ་ཚོས་ལ་ཐིགང་
ཐིག་ལེ་ལ་ཐིག།ཐིག་ལེ་ཚོས་ཀྱི་སྐུ་དང་མ་བྲ་ཆྱི་དང་པར་བསམས་སྟེའདི་སྐད་ཅེས་བརྗོད་

A Ritual Manual of the Fifty-eight Wrathful Deities

པར་བྱའོ།(18b4)དེ་ནས་བུ་ཏྲེང་ཐམས་ཅད་ཀུན་བདག་གི་ཕྱགས་གར་བསྒྲུབ་ནི།ཐུང་ཐུང་
ཞེས་ནི་རབ་བརྫོད་དེ།འདུས་པ་དེར་ནི་ཅི་བདེར་སྦྱིན།། །།(18b5)ན་མོ་དེ་ཡོ་ན་ཉིད་ཀྱི་སྐྱང་
བ་དཀའ་པ་རྒྱན་གི་བསྐོམ་ཐབས་རྫོགས་སོ།།

(31) །།དེ་སྐྱར་དཀྱིལ་འཁོར་གསལ་བར་བསྐྱེད་ནས།(18b6)དཀ་ནི་འཇིགས་བྱེད་ཆེན་པོའི་
དཀྱིལ་འཁོར་རྣམས་སྨྲན་དུང་བར་བུ་སྟེ།དེ་ཡང་རྒྱུད་ལས་འདི་སྐད་ཅེས་བརྫོད་པར་བྱའོ།།
ཚོགས་རྗེ་(18b7)ཚོགས་བདག་དཔལ་དང་ལྷན་འཇིགས་བྱེད་འཇིགས་འདུལ་འཇིགས་པའི་
རྒྱབས་རྡོ་རྗེ་ཁྲག་ཐུང་གཤེགས་སུ་གསོལ་ཐོད་དུས་(19a1)ཀ།།འབར་བའི་དཀྱིལ་འཁོར་ནས་
།དཀང་།ཁཾན་འགྲོའི་ཚོགས་དང་ལོང་སྦྱོང་ཅིང་གདུག་པ་མ་ལུས་འདུལ་མཛད་པ།ཚོགས་(19
a2)ཀྱི་སྟོབས་ནི་དཔོན་གཤེགས་སུ་གསོལ།ཡེ་ཤེས་ཐོ་གས་པའི་ཁྱད་བར་དུ་སྦྱལ་པ་མང་པོའི་
ཚོགས་དང་སྤྲུལ་ནི་ཕྱག་བགྱི་སྟེ།ཡང་(19a3)འདི་སྐད་ཅེས་བརྫོད་པར་བུ་འོ་བདག
ཐྱེད་ཕྱགས་བྱལ་དོན་དས་ཐྱགས་རྒྱུད་ཅིངཁྱམས་དང་སྟེང་རྗེ་འི་དགྲ་རྦུན་ཀྱི་མནའ་ཡེད་
གདུག་པའ་(19a4)འདུལ་ཕྱེར་དུས་ལས་ཀྱི་འད་བའི།འཇིགས་བྱེད་དེ་དུ་ཀ་ལ་ཕྱག་འཆལ་
ལོ།ཁྲ་མོ་དབང་ཕྱག་སྐུ་ལ་ཉེར་གནས་ཤིབ་ཐབས་དང་(19a5)ཤེས་རབ་འབར་བའི་དཀྱིལ་
འཁོར་ནས།མཁའ་མགྲ་ཀྱི་བཞད་འབར་བའི་སྟྱིན་འགྲོ་།གདུག་པ་འདུལ་མཛད་ཁྱོང་ལ་
ཕྱག(19a6)འཆལ་ལོ།ནས་ཀའི་ལུས་ཅན་གར་ཡང་ཐོགས་ཐྱེད་ཀྱིང་འདོང་ཀྲུར་བསྐྱར་བའི་
གཟུགས་ཅན་འཕུལ་མོ་ཆེན་སྟེང་ཁྱམས་མའི་ཁྱལ་(19a7)ཁྱལ་གིས་གྲོགས་མཛད་མ་ཁྱི་
ནང་མཁའ་འགྲོའི་ཚོགས་ལ་ཕྱག་འཆལ་ལོ།

(32)དེ་སྐྱར་ཕྱག་བགྱིས་ནས་གེ་ནི་བཧྟན་བར་(19b1)བཞུགས་སུ་གསོལ་ནས་དེ་ལ་འདི་
སྐྱད་ཅེས་བརྫོད་པར་བུ་འོ་རབ་ནི་མཆོན་མའི་དུས་ནི་འདི་ཉིད་དུ་ཀོ་རྗེ་ཚོགས་ཀུན་དགྱིས་
པར་(19b2)བསྒྲུབས་ལགས་ཀྱིས་གར་གི་དབང་ཕྱག་དགྱིས་ཤིང་བཞུགས་སུ་གསོལ།

(33)དེ་སྐྱར་བཧྟན་བར་བཞུགས་སུ་གསོལ་ནས་དེ་སྨན་(19b3)པན་ཚ་ཨ་འབྲི་ཏྲས་
མཆོད་པ་དབུལ་བར་བུ་སྟེ།ལ་འདི་སྐྱད་ཅེས་བརྫོད་པར་བྱའོ།ཚོགས་རྗེ་ཚོགས་བདག
དཔལ་ཆེན་དེ་དུ་ཀ།།(19b4)འབར་བའི་རྒྱལ་པོ་ཁྲག་འཐུང་ལྷ་རྣམས་ལ་རྣམ་དག་བདུད་རྩི་
དམ་ཚིག་མཆོད་པའ་འབུལ་ཕུལས་རྗེ་ཆེར་དགྱེངས་དབང་དང་(19b5)དངོས་གྲུབ་གསོལ།

88

ཨོཾ་ཧྲུང་དྲེས་མ་ཡུ་ཧྲུང་དྲེ༔ ཤ་ཧྲུག་པའི་ཆེན་སྐུ་དང་གཉིས་ཀྱེང་དོན་གཅིག་པ་འབད་(19b6)གྲོ་ཏེ་ཤྲ་རེ་ལས་བསྐྱེགས་ཡུམ་རྣམས་ལ་རྣམ་དག་བདུད་ཙི་དང་ཆོས་དགྱེས་མཆོད་དབུལ། ཕུགས་ཏེ་ཆེར་དགོང་དབང་དང་དངོས་(19b7)གྲུབ་གསོལ་ཨོཾ་ས་མ་ཡུ་ཧྲུངས་མ་ཡུ་ཨོཾ་ཁེ་ཤ་ཧྲུངས་མ་ཡུ་ཧྲག་ཤ་ཧྲུག་ལ་ལ་ལ་ཧྲུག་མཐིང་གའི་མཆོག་རྣམས་(20a1)༑༑ཀྲཱ་ཏཱ་གསང་བའི་ཡུམ་ཀྱི་ལུ་རེ་ལས་བསྐྱེགས་པུ་མེན་བརྒྱུད་རྣམས་ལས་རྣམ་དག་བདུད་ཙི་དང་ཆོ་ག་དགྱེས་མཆོད་འབུལ།(20a2)ཕུགས་ཏེ་ཆེར་དགོང་དབང་དང་དངོས་གྲུབ་གསོལ་ཏོ༔ ཏེ་མགོ་སྣན་ཟ་བྱེད་མཆེག་གཤོག་ཅན་སིང་ཏུ་ལས་བསྐྱེགས་པུ་མེན་བརྒྱུད་(20a3)རྣམས་ལ། རྣམ་དག་བདུད་ཙི་དང་ཆོག་དགྱེས་མཆོད་འབུལ་ཕུགས་ཏེ་ཆེར་དགོངས་དབང་དང་ངོས་གྲུབ་གསོལ་སྲི་རའི་སྲིང་འཛིན་(20a4)ཙི་སྲོམ་དག་ཆོག་དབང་བྱེད་མགགོང་མོ་ལས་བསྐྱེགས་སྲྱོ་བཞི་ནེ་འགྲོ་མོ་ལ་རྣམ་དག་བདུད་ཙི་དང་ཆོག་དགྱེས་མཆོད་འབུལ་ཕུགས་(20a5)ཏེ་ཆེ་དགོངས་དབང་དང་དངོས་གྲུབ་གསོལ་འདབལ་ཆེན་ཁྲི་ནང་བ་ཇཱ་ར་ལི་མ་ལ་ཁ་འགྲོ་ཕུགས་བསྐྱལ་མ་སྲིང་རྒྱན་མཚོ་ལ་རྣམས་(20a6)དག་བདུད་ཙི་དང་ཆོག་དགྱེས་མཆོད་འབུལ་ཕུགས་ཏེ་ཆེར་སྐོངས་དབང་དང་དངོས་གྲུབ་གསོལ་ཨོཾ་ཨེ་ཤ་ཧྲུ་ཧྲེ་ཤ་ཧྲུགས་མ་ཡུ་བག་(20a7)ཤ་ཧྲུག་ལ་ལ་ལ་ཀ་རཱོ་ཁ་བིཥྞ་པན་ཙ་ཨ་འབྲེ་ཧྲས་མ་མཆོད་པའི་གོང་དུ་འབར་བའི་གར་དང་ཕྱག་རྒྱའི་འབྱུང་སྟེ།

འབར་བའི་གར་དང་ཕྱག་རྒྱའི་འབྱུང་སྟེ།

(34)དེ་ལ་འདི་སྐ་ཅེས་(20b1)བརྗོད་པར་བྱ་བོ༔ཀྀ་ཨུ་རེ་བན་དྷ་དམར་ཐྲོས་དགྲུག་སྲོ་ཅེ་ཨུ་རེ་མདའ་གཞུན་འགྱེངས་མ་སེ་རགཱ་སྲ་མོ་ཚུ་སྲིན་རྒྱལ་མཆན་དམར་པའི་ཏུ་ཏྲི་ཨྥ་(20b2)རྫོ་འཕུར་གསན་སྱུ་ཀ་དམར་སེར་ཐྲེ་མཐུག་ལྒ་ཀགས་མ་ཏུང་དམར་ཁྲག་འཐུང་ལྷུངས་ལྷ་ཤ་མཐིང་ནག་ཏྲི་སྟེང་སྣ་རྩན་ཏུ་སེར་སྐུ་ཏྲི་ལུས་(20b3)མགོ་ལ་སྐྲ་ལད་པའི་སྲི་དབུང་འབར་བའི་སྲོང་དགྱལ་ནཱ་ཡེ་ཤེས་སྐུ་མཆོག་འཇིགས་བྱེད་རྒྱན་གྱིས་བཞག་འཕྲིན་ལས་རྫོགས་མཛད་(20b4)གྲུབ་པའི་དཔའ་གསུམ་དུ་སྲྱོག་སིང་ཀ་གཱ་རོ་སྨོལ་མར་སེར་བྱུ་ཁྲི་གནས་སླར་སྲོལ་མར་ལྷགས་ཁྲི་ཀ་ཁྲེས་ལྷ་གནག་མོ་ལྤཱ་ཧྲ་ན་འདུལ་དེ་མཐིང་(20b5)ཀ་ཁྲི་བཀྲི་ཏུ་དམར་མགྲིན་དམར་ཁྲག་འཐུང་ལྷུད་ཀང་ཀ་སྐུ་བན་སླར་མགོ་རེ་ངས་ཁ་ཁ་རོ་བན་གྱི་གནག་ཨུ་ལུ་རྫ་ཏྲེ་མཐིང་ཚོགས་ལུག།(20b6)མཆན་མར་ཏྲོག་པའི་ཏུག་སེལ་ཅིན་རྣམ་པར་དག་

པའི་བདུད་རྩེར་སྤྲོ་རྡ་ཁྲོར་དང་བསྐལ་བའི་བདུད་རྩེ་མཆོག་རྣམས་ཀྱིས་འཕུ་མེན་རྒྱུན་(20
b7)མཆོ་འི་ཐུགས་དམ་སྐོངས་འགྱུར་ཅིག་འཇའ་འཇ་ཏུ་གདོང་ལྕགས་ཀྱུ་མདའལ་མོ་ཐགས་
གདོང་ཞགས་པ་མགྲོ་ཀ་ར་གདོང་་(21a1)༢༠།།ཤུགས་སྐྲོག་མདགཀས་ཀྱི་པ་ལ་ཁྲི་གདོང་དུལ་
ཅེན་མགགཞན་ཡང་ཕུ་མེན་རྒྱ་མཆོ་མཁའ་འགྲོའི་ཆོགས།།ཏུར་ཁྱོད་(21a2)གསར་རྙིང་
གཉས་ནས་བཞིངས་པར་བསྐུལ་སྐྱལ་བའི་སྐུས་འདུལ་སྩ་འཆོགས་སྐྱུར་བསྟོན་ཅིད་འབར་
བའི་སྐུ་མཆོག་བདག་ལ་བསྟུན་ཏུ་(21a3)གསོལ་སྟོརད་དང་བསྐོལ་བའི་བདུད་རྩེའི་མཆོག་
རྣམས་ཀྱིས་རྗེ་རྗེ་ལས་ཀུན་མ་ལུས་གྲུབ་པར་མཛོད།

(35)དེ་ནི་འཛིགས་ཏེད་ཆེན་པོའི་དཀྱིལ་(21a4)འཁོར་རྣམས་ལ་མཐོལ་བཤགས་བཏོད་
པ་དཔལ་བཟ་བྱ་སྟེ།།དེ་ལ་འདི་སྐད་ཅེས་བཙོད་པར་བྱ་བོཀྵ་བ་འཁང་དམས་ཆོས་ཀྱི་དོན་
མ་རྟོགས།།(21a5)བསྒོམ་བྲ་ཡུན་འབྱུངས་ཡི་དགས་སྤ་ཀྱི་གསལ།།ཤི་ཞུ་ཆུངས་བས་སྐོབས་
དཔོན་སྐུ་མ་མཉེས་བསྒྲུང་འཆམས་འདགས་པའི་རོངས་བགྱིས་བཙོད་པར་(21a6)གསོལ།།
(36)གཉིས་ལྡན་ཕྱན་ཕྱག་རྒྱན་གཏུམས་པ་ལས།།འབག་ཆགས་བཟེག་པའི་ཁྲི་འཁུང་།།ཕྲིན་མོངས་
ཁྲོད་ཀྱི་རྣམ་རྟོག་བཟེགཀྵས་རངས་(21a7)ཞེས་བཙོད་པས་ཁྲི་འི་དཀྱིལ་འཁོར་ཏུ་འགྱུརད་ཏེ
།ཁྲིན་མོངས་པའི་བག་ཆགས་ཐམས་ཅད་བསྒགས་སྤང་ས་པར་བསམ་མོ།ཇུ་རྒྱ་གྲས་དབང་
ཆེན་(21b1)གཏུམས་པ་ལ་ལྐུང་ནག་དཀྱིལ་འཁོར་བདག་ཞིད་ཅེ།ཐམས་ཅད་འདེགས་པའི་
སྟོབས་དང་སྟན་ཁྲིན་མོངས་ཁྲོད་ཀྱི་རྣམ་རྟོག་འབྱད་(21b2)ཡང་ཡང་ཞེས་བཙོད་པསྐྲུང་
གི་དཀྱིལ་འཁོར་ཆེན་པོར་འགྱུརད་ཏེ།ཁྱིས་བཞེགས་པའི་ཐབ་ལ་ཐམས་ཅད་གཡེངས་པར་
བསམ་མོ།ཁང་ཁང་(21b3)ཞེས་བཙོད་པས་ཡི་གི་ཁང་སྤོ་སྐ་ལས་རྒྱ་འི་དཀྱིལ་འཁོར་ཏུ་
འགྱུརད་ཏེ།སྐྲུང་གིས་བཏེགས་གཏོར་བའི་ལྐ་མ་ཐམས་ཅད་བརྒུལ་བཀལ་བར་(21b4)
བསམ་མོ།།ཡི་གི་ཐུགས་རྗེའི་དཀྱིལ་འཁོར་ལསབག་ཆགས་འཇུ་བའི་རྒྱ་འབྱུང་བྲ་ཧྲིན་མོངས་
ཁྲིད་ཀྱི་རྣམ་རྟོག་འབྱུད་་སྤྲ་(21b5)བག་ཆགས་སྤུངས་ནས་ཏེ་ལ་འདི་སྐད་ཅེས་བཙོད་
པར་བྱ་བོ་དང་བོར་བདག་ཞིད་རྟོག་བསྒོམ་བསྐུལ་ཏེ་ནས་གཉིས་ཁྲིད་ལྟོ་ཞོས་ནེ།(21b6)སྐོ
ངན་འཛིག་རྟེན་སྟིང་རེ་རྟེ་གཉིས་སུ་ཁྱིད་པར་བསྐལ་བར་བྱའ།
(37)དེ་ནི་ལམ་རྒྱུད་སྤ་བཀོད་པར་བྱ་སྟེ།དེ་ལ་འདི་སྐད་ཅེས་བཙོད་པར་བྱ་བོ(21b7)སྐྱི་

འོར་ཨྠོན་བར་དུ་ངསྟར་ཨམཱལྟེ་བར་སྟུ་ལྟྲེ་ལ་དུ་དེ་སྲར་ལས་རྒྱུད་ལུའི་སྟེང་པོ་གསལ་བར་ བགོད་ནས་དེ་ལ་(22a1)༄༄་ལ་འདི་སྲང་ཅེས་བརྗོད་པར་བྱའོ།།སྟ་ན་འི་གནས་མཆོག་ ཁྱད་བར་དུ་སྲགས་ཀྱི་ཡི་གེ་ཨོྠ་བསྒྱོམས་པས་རྣམ་པར་སྣང་(21a2)མཛད་སྐུར་འགྱུར་ན། བསད་པ་ཉྱེད་ཀྱིས་འྠོད་མ་འཇིགས་ས་འི་གནས་མཆོག་ཁྱད་བར་དུ་སྲགས་ཀྱི་ཡི་གེ་ཏུཾ་ བསྒྱོམས་པས་རྟོ་རྗེ་(21a3)སེམས་པའི་སྐུར་འགྱུར་ནས་བསད་པ་ཉྱེད་ཀྱིས་འྠོད་མ་འཇིགས་ སྟ་ན་འི་གནས་མཆོག་ཁྱད་བར་དུ་སྲགས་ཀྱི་ཡི་གེ་སྲ་བསྒྱོམས་པས།(21a4)རིན་ཅེན་འབྱུང་ སྲན་སྐུར་འགྱུར་ནས་བསད་པ་ཉྱེད་ཀྱིས་འྠོད་མ་འཇིགས་ས་ན་འི་གནས་མཆོག་ཁྱད་པར་དུ། སྲགས་ཀྱི་ཡི་གེ་ཨོྠ་བསྒྱོམས་པས།(22a5)སྣང་བ་མཐའ་ཡས་སྐུར་འགྱུར་ག་བསད་པ་ཉྱེད་ ཀྱིས་འྠོད་མ་འཇིགས་ས་འི་གནས་མཆོག་ཁྱད་བར་དུ་སྲགས་ཀྱི་ཡི་གེ་ཏུ་བསྒྱོམས་པས།(22 a5)རྟོན་ཡོད་གྲུབ་པའི་སྐུར་འགྱུར་ག་བསད་པ་ཉྱེད་པ་ཉྱེད་ཀྱིས་འྠོད་མ་འཇིགས་རྣམ་ཤེས་ གནས་པའི་ཕྱང་པོ་སྲའབུ་ཏུ་སྲ་ལ་སྔྱེན་བར་བྱེད།

(38)(22a6)དེ་ནས་སྲོབས་དཔོན་གྱིས་ཞིང་འཕྱར་མཆོག་འདུལ་མཆོག་འཕེན་གྱིས་གདི་ཟྲ་ འི་དཀྱིལ་དུ་མཁས་པས་བཞགང་རྒྱལ་ལན་(22b1)གྱིས་འདུ་བྱེད་བསྒྱོམསྟུ་ཨ་གྱུར་ནས་ རྣམ་པར་དགའ་དྱེངས་སུ་ཐིམ་ནས་ཕྱག་རྒྱར་གསལ་སྐྱར་འཕྱར་རོན་རེར་འརྲོ་བས་བརྟིད། (22b2)གཙུག་དུ་རྣམ་པར་རྒྱལ་ནྲ་བསྒྱམཌོ་མཆར་ངན་འརྲོ་ཐ་ར་ད་པ་འི་ལས༽ལྱེ་ནས་སྐྱེ་ ཉྱེད་དེ་བཞིན་ཉྱེད༽སྟོར་བསྒྱལ་བྱ་བས།(22b3)གུན་བྱས་ཡད་རྟ་ལ་ཆ་ཚོམ་ཡང་བྱས་པ་ཉྱེད། ༽སྲུ་མར་སྲང་བ་དཔྱེག་གཡོར་ཚུ་ལ།། །།རྗོགས་སྟོ།།

(39)(22b4)ཨྠོ་བ་རྲ་ཨ་བྱེ་ཉྱེན་ཙ་ཏུཾཨྠོ་འབུ་ཏ་ཨ་བཉྱེ་ཉྱེན་ཙ་ཨྠྠོ་རད་ན་ཨ་བྱེ་ཉྱེན་ཙ་ ཏུཨྠོ་པད་མ་ཨ་བྱེ་ཉྱེན་ཙ་ཏྱེཨྠོ་གར་མ་ཨ་བྱེ་ཉྱེན་ཙ་ཨ།(22b5)ཨྠོ་འབུ་ད་སྲུད་ཏུ་ཨ་བྱེ་ ཉྱེན་ཙ་ཨྠོཨྠོ་བ་རྲ་སྲུ་ད་ཨ་བྱེ་ཉྱེན་ཙ་ཏུཨྠོ་རད་ན་སྲུད་ཏུ་ཨ་བྱེ་ཉྱེན་ཙ་ཏུཨྠོ་པད་མ་སྲུད་ ཏུ་ཨ་བྱེ་ཉྱེན་ཙ་ཏྱེཨྠོ(22b6)གར་མ་སྲུད་ད་ཨ་བྱེ་ཉྱེན་ཙ་ཨཨྠོ་བ་རྲ་ན་ན་ཨ་བྱེ་ཉྱེན་ཙ་ཧྠུ ཁྲུ་ཏྱེ་ཨཨྠོ་བ་རྲ་ཙ་གྲ་ཨཏྱེ་ཉྱེན་ཙ་ཧྠུཨྠོ་གར་མ་ཨ་བྱེ་ཉྱེན་ཙ་ཧྠུ་ཨ།(22b7)ཨྠོ་བ་རྲ་ཏྱེ་པ་ ཏྱེ་ཊ་ཨ་བྱེ་ཉྱེན་ཙ་ཨྠོ་ཨྠོ་ཨྠོཧྠུ་ཧྠུ་ཧྠུཊུ་ཊུ་ཊུཊི་ཏྱེ་ཏྱེ༽ཁ་ལ་ཨ་ཨཨྠོ་བ་རྲ་རད་ན་ཨ་བྱེ་ཉྱེན་ཙ

A Ritual Manual of the Fifty-eight Wrathful Deities

ཏུ༔ཨོཾ་བཛྲ་ཏ་ཐཱ་ག་ཏ་ཧ྄ཱུར་ན་ལ་(22b8)ཏྲེ་ཤིན་ཙ་ཨོཾ་ཨོཾ་རད་ན་རད་ན་ཙུ་ལ་ཏྲི་ཤིན་ཙ་ཏུ ཨོཾ་པད་མ་ཧཱ་ར་ཙུ་ཏྲི་ཤིན་ཙ་ཏྲི་ཨོཾ་ཀཱར་མ་ད་ར་ཙུ་ཏྲི་ཤིན་ཙ་ཨཱ།།

92

Wallpainting of the Fifty-eight Wrathful Deities (Tukuche, Nepal)

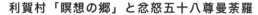

利賀村「瞑想の郷」と忿怒五十八尊曼荼羅

　富山県南砺市利賀村の「瞑想の郷」は、チベット・ネパール仏教美術に特化した国内唯一の公立のテーマパークである。現在、「瞑想の郷」は利賀ふるさと財団によって運営されている。

　同館の主要な展示物は、４メートル四方の巨大な仏教絵画６点である。それらは①寂静四十二尊曼荼羅、②忿怒五十八尊曼荼羅、③阿弥陀如来と極楽浄土図、④十一面千手観音(ソンツェンガムポ王流)[以上「瞑想の館」]、⑤金剛界曼荼羅、⑥胎蔵曼荼羅[以上「瞑想美の館」]である。このうち②忿怒五十八尊曼荼羅を、本書の図版として使用している。

　これらは旧利賀村(南砺市に合併)の姉妹村、ネパールの下ムスタンにあるツクチェ村出身のタカリ族の仏画家、サシ・ドジ・トラチャン氏によって描かれた。彼は、ツクチェのチベット仏教ニンマ派の在家密教行者(ガクパ)の

家系に生まれ、父親から仏画の手ほどきを受けた後、さらに数人の師匠に就いてチベット仏画を学んだ。とくにルンビニのチベット寺とボードナートのチャムチェン・ゴムパ（大弥勒寺）の住職を務めた、故サキャ・チョギェー・ティチェン・リンポチェ（1920-2007）を根本ラマとした。

　巨大な仏画が完成すると、村はこれを収納する「瞑想の館」の建設に着手し、さらにレストランと宿泊施設、曼荼羅花壇などが造られた。さらに2003年には、ネパール政府観光局から「名誉観光事務所」に認定されている。

　著者は1989年にサシ氏が初めて来日した時から、このプロジェクトに関わり、1997年には同館の主任学芸員（非常勤）に任命された。さらに2006年には、『ヴァジュラーヴァリー』と「ミトラ百種」に基づくCG曼荼羅が、常設展示に加えられた。

　「瞑想の郷」は水曜日を除く毎日営業しているが、豪雪地帯にあるため、冬期（12月～3月）は休業している。

　寂静忿怒百尊は、数多いニンマ派の図像の中でも、最も普及している画題であり、現在でもチベット文化圏の至る所で、その作例を見ることができる。

　寂静忿怒百尊は、しばしば寂静四十二尊と忿怒五十八尊を描いた二幅のタンカ・セットとして描かれるが、一幅のタンカに寂静四十二尊と忿怒五十八尊を、すべて描いた作品もある。このような構成は、後に成立したニンマ派の埋蔵教法（テルマ）に説かれるものである。

　新訳諸派の曼荼羅とは異なり、寂静忿怒百尊の曼荼羅では、多くの場合、曼荼羅の方形の楼閣と外側の円形の守護輪が描かれない。そこで「瞑想の郷」所蔵の忿怒五十八尊曼荼羅（本書カバー図版）のような作例は、ニンマ派のラマから正統的な図像でないと批判されることがある。

　しかし本作品のように、方形の楼閣と円形の守護輪を伴った作例も、僅かではあるが存在する。一例を挙げると、ラヴィクマール・コレクションの作

品（Pratapaditya Pal: *Tibetan Paintings*, Sotheby 1984, pl. 102）は、一幅のタンカに、新訳派の曼荼羅のような円形の守護輪と方形の楼閣を伴う、寂静四十二尊（上部）と忿怒五十八尊（下部）の曼荼羅が描かれている。さらに敦煌のペリオ・コレクションから発見された寂静四十二尊の現存最古の作例(EO 1144; ninth century) も、簡略化された方形の楼閣の中に尊格を描いている。

さらに下ムスタンにおいても、カクベニ村の過街塔の天井には、方形の楼閣と円形の守護輪を伴った寂静四十二尊と忿怒五十八尊の曼荼羅が描かれている。（99頁、101頁写真）

なお本曼荼羅の作者は、「瞑想の郷」の曼荼羅絵師、他ならぬサシ・ドジ・トラチャンの父親、カマル・ドジ・トラチャンである。

したがって、方形の楼閣と円形の守護輪を伴う忿怒五十八尊曼荼羅は、作例としては稀であるが、何らかの伝統に基づくと考えられるのである。

「瞑想の郷」
所在地：〒939-2514 富山県南砺市利賀村上畠１０１
電話番号：0763-68-2324
「利賀ふるさと財団」（休業中の連絡先）
所在地：〒939-2513 富山県南砺市利賀村上百瀬４８２
電話番号：0763-68-2131

Toga Meditation Museum and Maṇḍala of the Fifty-eight Wrathful Deities

The Creation of Maṇḍala of the Forty-eight Peaceful Deities (1990).

Toga Meditation Museum (Meisō no Sato) is a unique theme park focusing on Tibeto-Nepalese Buddhist art that was established by a local government body in Toyama prefecture, Japan. The museum is now managed by a quasi-public corporation named Toga Furusato Foundation.

The main exhibits in Toga Meditation Museum are six Buddhist paintings: (1) Maṇḍala of the Forty-two peaceful deities, (2) Maṇḍala of the fifty-eight wrathful deities, (3) Amitābha and his pure land, (4) One-thousand-armed Avalokiteśvara in the King Sroṅ-btsan-sgam-po style, (5) Garbha-maṇḍala, and (6) Vajradhātu-maṇḍala, each measuring 4 square metres. The maṇḍala of the

97

A Ritual Manual of the Fifty-eight Wrathful Deities

Fifty-eight wrathful deities has been used on the cover of this book.

The paintings were produced in Toga village by Mr. Sashi Dhoj Tulachan, a Thakali Buddhist painter from Toga's sister village, Tukuche in lower Mustang, Nepal. He was born into a *sNgag pa* family, lay practitioners of the rÑiṅ-ma school of Tibetan Buddhism, in Tukuche. After having received basic training as a Buddhist painter from his father, he studied Buddhist painting under several teachers. In particular, the late Sakya bco brgyad khri chen (1920-2007), the abbot of the Tibetan Buddhist Temple in Lumbini and Byams chen dgon pa at Bodhnath, was his root teacher (*rtsa ba'i bla ma*).

After the completion of the paintings, Toga village constructed a museum to enshrine them. Later, a restaurant, a guesthouse, and a beautiful garden in the shape of a maṇḍala were added. In 2003, this museum was officially recognized by the Nepalese Government as an Honorary Representative of the Nepal Tourism Board.

I have been participating in the project since the painter's first visit to Toga in 1989, and I was appointed chief curator of the museum in 1997. In July 2006, the CG maṇḍalas of the *Vajrāvalī* and Mitra brgya rtsa sets were opened to the public as permanent exhibits.

The museum is open daily except on Wednesdays and is closed during the winter (December-March) since it is located in an area with heavy snowfall.

The One hundred peaceful and wrathful deities (*źi khro*) are the most popular subject in the rich iconography of the rÑiṅ-ma school. Even today, we can see numerous examples throughout the Tibetan cultural region.

The Maṇḍala of the Forty-two Peaceful Deities, Kagbeni, Nepal. (1994)

They are often represented in sets of two thangkas depicting the Forty-two peaceful and Fifty-eight wrathful deities separately, but in some examples all one hundred deities have been depicted in a single thangka. This type of composition is described in later works among the treasure-texts (*gter ma*) of

A Ritual Manual of the Fifty-eight Wrathful Deities

the rÑiṅ-ma school.

In contrast to the maṇḍalas of new tantric schools, in many cases the maṇḍalas of the One hundred peaceful and wrathful deities do not have a square pavilion and outer protective circles. Consequently, the maṇḍala of the Fifty-eight wrathful deities of Toga Meditation Museum that has been used for the cover of this book is sometimes criticized as unorthodox by lamas of the rÑiṅ-ma school.

However, we can find examples of the maṇḍala of the One hundred peaceful and wrathful deities with a square pavilion and outer protective circles like the present work. For example, an example in the possession of the Ravi Kumar collection (Pratapaditya Pal, *Tibetan Paintings* [Sotheby, 1984], pl. 102) depicts the forty-two peaceful deities (top) and the fifty-eight wrathful deities (bottom) in square pavilions and outer protective circles just like the new tantric schools of Tibetan Buddhism. And the earliest extant example of the Forty-two peaceful deities discovered at Dunhuang and preserved in the Pelliot collection (EO 1144; ninth century) also has a square pavilion in an abridged form.

In lower Mustang, too, I found a example of maṇḍalas of the Forty-two peaceful deities and Fifty-eight wrathful deities with a square pavilion and outer protective circles on the ceiling of the entrance gate to Kagbeni village (see fig. on p. 99, 101). The painter of this maṇḍala was none other than Kamal Dhoj Tulachan, the father of our painter.

Therefore, the maṇḍala of the Fifty-eight wrathful deities with a square pavilion and outer protective circles, though rare, is confirmed to be based on tradition.

The Maṇḍala of the Fifty-eight Wrathful Deities, Kagbeni, Nepal. (1994)

Toga Meditation Museum

101 Uwabatake, Toga-mura, Nanto-City, Toyama, 939-2514 Japan.

Phone : +81- (0) 763-68-2324

Contact address during winter break:

Toga Furusato Foundation

482 Kami-momose, Toga-mura, Nanto City, Toyama, 939-2253 Japan.

Phone: +81- (0) 763-68-2131

ビブリオグラフィー（Bibliography）

【邦文】[Japanese]

ジャン・フランソワ・ジャリージュほか[Jarrige, J. F., et al.] 1994, 『西域美術　ギメ美術館ペリオ・コレクションⅠ』[Les Arts de L'Asie Centrale] （講談社） Tokyo: Kodansha Ltd.

金子英一[Kaneko, Eiichi] 1982,『古タントラ全集解題目録』[A complete catalogue of the *rÑiṅ ma rgyud 'bum*] （国書刊行会）Tokyo: Kokusho Kankōkai.

川崎信定[Kawasaki, Shinjō] 1989, 『原典訳　チベットの死者の書』[A Japanese Translation of the *Tibetan Book of the Dead* from Tibetan Original]. （筑摩書房）Tokyo: Chikumashobo.

田中公明[Tanaka, Kimiaki] 1986, 「敦煌出土のニンマ派密教典籍について」[On the Źi-khro literature discovered from Tun-huang]. 山口瑞鳳編『チベットの仏教と社会』[Buddhism and society in Tibet], 199–214. （春秋社）Tokyo: Shunjūsha.

— 1990. 『詳解河口慧海コレクション―チベット・ネパール仏教美術―』[A Catalogue of Ekai Kawaguchi's collection of Tibetan and Nepalese Buddhist Art] （佼成出版社）Tokyo: Kosei Publishing.

— 1998-2015, 『チベット仏教絵画集成』[Art of Thangka, from the Hahn Kwang-ho collection] （第1巻～第7巻）（ハンビッツ文化財団）Seoul: Hahn Cultural Foundation.

— 2000, 『敦煌　密教と美術』[Essays on Tantric Buddhism in Dunhuang: Its Art and Texts] （法藏館）Kyoto: Hōzōkan.

— 2010, 『インドにおける曼荼羅の成立と発展』[Genesis and Development of the Maṇḍala in India] （春秋社）Tokyo: Shunjūsha.

田中公明ほか[Tanaka, Kimiaki et al.] 1994, 『チベット生と死の文化』[Tibet, Culture of Birth and Death]（東京美術）Tokyo: Tokyo Bijutsu.

山口瑞鳳ほか［Yamaguchi, Zuiho et al.］1977-1988, 『スタイン蒐集チベット語文献解題目録』[A Catalogue of the Tibetan Manuscripts collected by Sir Aurel Stein]（第 1 分冊〜第12分冊）［Part 1-12］（東洋文庫）Tokyo: The Toyo Bunko.

【欧文】[Western Languages]

Dalton, Jacob & Van Shaik, Sam. 2006. *Tibetan Tantric Manuscripts from Dunhuang,* A Descriptive Catalogue of the Stein Collection at the British Library. Leiden: Brill.

Evans-Wentz, W. Y. 1927. *Tibetan Book of the Dead.* Oxford: Oxford University Press.

Tanaka, Kimiaki. 1992. "A Comparative Study of Esoteric Buddhist Manuscripts and Icons Discovered at Dun-huang." In *Tibetan Studies: Proceedings of the 5th Seminar of the International Association for Tibetan Studies, Narita 1989*, 275-279. Narita: Naritasan Shinshōji.

— 2018. *An Illustrated History of the Mandala*, From its Genesis to the Kālacakratantra. Somerville: Wisdom Publications.

Pal, Pratapaditya. 1984. *Tibetan Paintings.* London: Sotheby.

あとがき

　敦煌莫高窟の蔵経洞から厖大な文献と絵画類が発見されてから、120年が経過しようとしている。発見された資料は東洋学の各分野に新知見をもたらし、「敦煌学」と呼ばれる一分野が形成された。

　わが国でも敦煌学は、1960年から80年代にかけて隆盛を迎えた。しかし現在、少なくとも我々が関わってきた仏教に関しては、敦煌研究は一段落した観が否めない。とくに漢文仏典に関しては、カタログの刊行や画像データベースの公開により、研究はすでに成熟の域に達したといってよいであろう。

　いっぽう仏教美術に関しては、『西域美術』シリーズ(講談社)の刊行によって、スタイン・ペリオ両コレクションの全容が、わが国にも広く知られるようになった。

　しかし著者が2000年に刊行した『敦煌　密教と美術』(法藏館)は、わが国ではほとんど注目されず、忘れ去られたも同然になっていた。ところが拙著に収録した「寂静四十二尊」「蓮華部八尊曼荼羅」「胎蔵大日八大菩薩」の3編の論文が敦煌研究院の劉永増研究員によって中国語訳され、2002年から2010年にかけて『敦煌研究』に収録された。さらに2007年にイェール大学で開催された国際学会、Esoteric Buddhist Tradition in East Asia: Text, Ritual and Imageに参加し、敦煌研究院の王恵民氏らと名刺を交換したところ、敦煌研究院では研究員の間で、拙著が評判になっていることを知った。

　そこで2019年9月に、劉永増氏とともに四川大学蔵学研究所の霍巍教授を訪ね、同著を増補改訂のうえ、中国語版を刊行することで合意した。

　ただし前著では、第11章に収録した忿怒五十八尊の儀軌(IOL Tib J 332)のみは、予定された紙数を大幅に超過するため、チベット語テキストを収録することができなかった。そこで中国語版を刊行するにあたり、同文献のロー

マ字化テキストを増補するとともに、別途、日英二カ国語版の本書を刊行することにした。

　1959年のチベット動乱以後、チベット仏教ニンマ派が欧米に伝播し、知識人の関心を集めるようになった。そこでニンマ派の原初形態である吐蕃時代の古密教を知るかけがえのない資料である本文献の研究は、欧米におけるニンマ派研究に一石を投じるものになると考えたのである。

　大英図書館旧インド局図書室（IOL）所蔵のチベット語写本に関しては、大英図書館「国際敦煌プロジェクト」の協力を受けた。また文献概説の英文校閲は、畏友ロルフ・ギーブル氏にお願いした。いっぽうチベット語要旨の校閲は、チベット大学（サールナート）のチャンバサムテン教授のお手をわずらわせた。さらに本書の刊行を引き受けられた（有）渡辺出版の渡辺潔社長にも大変お世話になった。末筆となってはなはだ恐縮であるが、記して感謝の意を表させていただきたい。

2019年12月21日

著者。

Postscript

One hundred and twenty years have passed since the vast quantities of ancient documents and pictorial materials were discovered in the Library Cave of the Magao Grottoes near Dunhuang. These materials have had an enormous influence on subsequent East Asian studies, and a new branch of scholarship known as "Dunhuang studies" came into existence.

In Japan, Dunhuang studies peaked during the period from the 1960s to 1980s. Today, however, Dunhuang studies seems to have come to a standstill, at least in the area of Buddhist studies, with which this book is concerned. With regard to Chinese Buddhist texts, exhaustive catalogues and image databases of manuscripts have been made accessible to the public, and research has fully matured.

As for Buddhist art, the publication of *The Art of Central Asia* (1982-84), based on the Stein collection in the British Museum, and *Les arts de l'Asie centrale* (1994), based on the Pelliot collection in the Musée Guimet, both published by Kōdansha, revealed to Japanese researchers a full picture of the Stein and Pelliot collections.

However, my *Essays on Tantric Buddhism in Dunhuang: Its Art and Texts* (Hōzōkan, 2000) did not attract much attention and was largely forgotten in Japan. But Dr. Liu Yongzeng of the Dunhuang Research Academy translated three of the essays into Chinese, namely, those on the forty-two peaceful deities, the eight-deity maṇḍala of the Lotus family, and Vairocana and the eight great bodhisattvas from Dunhuang, and they appeared in the Academy's journal, *Dunhuang Yanjiu*, between 2002 and 2010. When I attended the international conference "Esoteric Buddhist Tradition in East Asia: Text, Ritual and Image" at Yale University in 2007, I met Dr. Wang Huimin from the Dunhuang Research Academy and learnt that, in contrast to Japan, my book had come to the notice of researchers at the Dunhuang Research Academy.

In September 2019, I visited Professor Huo Wei of Sichuan University in Chengdu together with Dr. Liu Yongzeng and reached an agreement to publish a revised and enlarged edition of my book in Chinese. In the original Japanese version, for reasons of space I had not been able to include the Tibetan text of IOL Tib J 332, the main subject of chapter 11. I accordingly added a transcription of IOL Tib J 332 for the Chinese edition. In addition, I decided to publish a Japanese-English bilingual monograph on the Fifty-eight wrathful deities from Dunhuang.

After the Tibetan uprising in 1959, the rÑiṅ ma school of Tibetan Buddhism was transmitted to the West and attracted the interest of scholars. Therefore, I anticipate that this study of the Fifty-eight wrathful deities during the Tufan dynasty of Tibet, a primitive form of the present-day rÑiṅ ma school, will have some impact on rÑiṅ ma studies in the West.

With regard to Tibetan manuscripts in the possession of the former Indian Office Library (IOL), I received the kind cooperation of the International Dunhuang Project at the British Museum. In addition, I would like to offer my heartful thanks to all those who have helped in the preparation of this publication, including Mr. Rolf Giebel, who assisted with the English translation and gave me helpful advice; Professor Jampa Samten of Central University of Tibetan Studies (Sarnath), who oversaw the Tibetan summary; and Mr. Kiyoshi Watanabe, the president of Watanabe Publishing Co., Ltd., who undertook to

A Ritual Manual of the Fifty-eight Wrathful Deities

publish this book with great care.

21/Dec/2019

Kimiaki TANAKA

著者略歴

田中公明（たなかきみあき）

　1955（昭和30）年、福岡県八幡市（現北九州市）生まれ。東京大学文学部卒（印度哲学専攻）、1984年同大学大学院博士課程満期退学。同大学文学部助手（文化交流）を経て、1988年（財）東方研究会［現（公財）中村元東方研究所］専任研究員。2008年、東京大学大学院より博士［文学］号を取得。2013年、学位論文『インドにおける曼荼羅の成立と発展』（春秋社）で鈴木学術財団特別賞を受賞。2018年にはWisdom Publicationsから、その英語版An Illustrated History of the Mandalaも刊行された。

　東京大学（1992, 1994〜1996, 2001〜2004年）、拓殖大学（1994, 1998年）、大正大学綜合佛教研究所（2016年）、高野山大学（2016年）等で非常勤講師、北京日本学研究センター短期派遣教授（2003, 2010年）を歴任。現在（2020年）、富山県南砺市利賀村「瞑想の郷」主任学芸員、チベット文化研究会副会長。東方学院（2001年〜）、慶應義塾大学（2001〜2020年）、東洋大学大学院（2017年〜）講師［いずれも非常勤］、ネパール留学（1988〜89年）、英国オックスフォード大学留学（1993年）。韓国ハンビッツ文化財団学術顧問（1997〜2015年）として、同財団の公式図録『チベット仏教絵画集成』第1巻〜第7巻（臨川書店）を編集。密教、仏教図像、チベット学に関する著訳書（共著を含む）58冊、論文とエッセイ約150点。

詳しくは個人HP
http://kimiakitanak.starfree.jp/を参照。

About the Author

Kimiaki TANAKA (b.1955, Fukuoka) is a research fellow at the Nakamura Hajime Eastern Institute, Tokyo. He studied Indian Philosophy and Sanskrit Philology at the University of Tokyo. He received a doctorate in literature from the University of Tokyo in 2008 for his dissertation entitled "Genesis and Development of the Maṇḍala in India." It was published in 2010 by Shunjūsha with financial support from the Japan Society for the Promotion of Science and was awarded the Suzuki Research Foundation Special Prize in 2013. In 2018, an English version of the dissertation, *An Illustrated History of the Mandala, From Its Genesis to the Kālacakratantra* was published from Wisdom Publications in USA.

He has been lecturer at the University of Tokyo, at Takushoku University, at the Institute for Comprehensive Studies of Buddhism, Taisho University (Genesis and Development of the Mandala) and at Koyasan University (Genesis and Development of the Mandala), teaching Tibetan as well as courses on Buddhism. He studied abroad as a visiting research fellow (1988-89) at Nepal Research Centre (Kathmandu) and held a Spalding Visiting Fellowship at Oxford University (Wolfson College) in 1993. As a visiting professor, he gave lectures on Sino-Japanese cultural exchange at Beijing Centre for Japanese Studies in 2003 and 2010.

From 1997 to 2015, he was the academic consultant to the Hahn Cultural Foundation (Seoul) and completed 7 vol. catalogue of their collection of Tibetan art entitled *Art of Thangka*. He is presently (2020) lecturer at Tōhō Gakuin, in Art History at Keio University (Buddhist Iconography) and in graduate course at Toyo University (Esoteric Buddhism). He is also chief curator of the Toga Meditation Museum in Toyama prefecture, the Vice-President of the Tibet

A Ritual Manual of the Fifty-eight Wrathful Deities

Culture Centre International in Tokyo. He has published more than 58 books and 150 articles (including essays) on Esoteric Buddhism, Buddhist Iconography and Tibetan art.

http://kimiakitanak.starfree.jp/

敦煌出土　忿怒五十八尊儀軌

令和2年6月27日　第一刷発行

著　者　田中公明

発行者　渡辺 潔

発行所　有限会社渡辺出版

〒113-0033

東京都文京区本郷5丁目18番19号

電話　03-3811-5447

振替　00150-8-15495

印刷所　シナノ書籍印刷株式会社

©Kimiaki TANAKA 2020 Printed in Japan
ISBN978-4-902119-32-9

A Ritual Manual
of the Fifty-eight Wrathful Deities
from Dunhuang
— Introduction, Tibetan Text and Related Studies —

Date of Publication: 27 June 2020

Author: Kimiaki Tanaka

Publisher: Watanabe Publishing Co., Ltd.

5-18-19 Hongo, Bunkyo-ku

Tokyo 113-0033 Japan

tel/fax: 03-3811-5447

e-mail: watanabe.com@bloom.ocn.ne.jp

Printer: SHINANO BOOK PRINTING Co., Ltd.

Distributor (Outside of Japan): Vajra Publications,

Jyatha, Thamel, P.O. Box : 21779, Kathmandu, Nepal

tel/fax: 977-1-4220562

e-mail: vajrabooks@hotmail.com

©Kimiaki TANAKA 2020 Printed in Japan
ISBN978-4-902119-32-9